I0478711

TRAILER PARK PEOPLE

Photographs by

Tom Sundro Lewis

Interviews and editing by

Drea Knufken

The American cultural stereotype might equate trailers with survival, but here in Boulder, people are choosing the trailer park as a way to thrive. "Trailer Park People" explores the value of downsizing, settling in, growing a garden, creating community, and investing in less.

When we took a look at this mobile home park in the heart of Boulder, Colorado, we found a hub of conscious living. By choosing a tiny space, residents find they can live more sustainably and simply, in one of America's most beautiful cities.

It begs consideration of the question: Which is crazier, pursuing a large mansion and more stuff, or making the decision to live with less? For these residents, at least, the answer is obvious.

Drea Knufken and Tom Sundro Lewis

Funding has been made possible, in part, by a grant from the Puffin Foundation

We'd like to acknowledge everyone who has helped in making this project a reality. Without all the time and consideration that each person gave so willingly to be interviewed and photographed, this certainly would not have happened. Thank you all, so very much.

We'd like to thank Gene Langlois, in particular, for all his encouragement to begin something like this in the first place. Like his garden, it just grew and grew!

We'd also like to thank all our friends and family for their helpful suggestions and support.

And last but not least, thanks goes to the Puffin Foundation for its financial assistance.

Without all of you, what kind of a community would we have?

Tom Sundro Lewis and Drea Knufken

I ended up here because I ran out of money. It's the best move I ever made. I've been in the park for a total of 25 years.

I never quite got caught up with "more is better" mentality. I didn't put myself in an economic condition where I had to lie or cheat or steal. I didn't get caught in the system. One day, I decided to stop watching TV, and found that I had all this time.

I went back to school. I learned massage and woodworking and gardening. I had time to play. It inspired me to be creative.

Finally, I found out what I wanted. I just wanted to blossom.

-G.

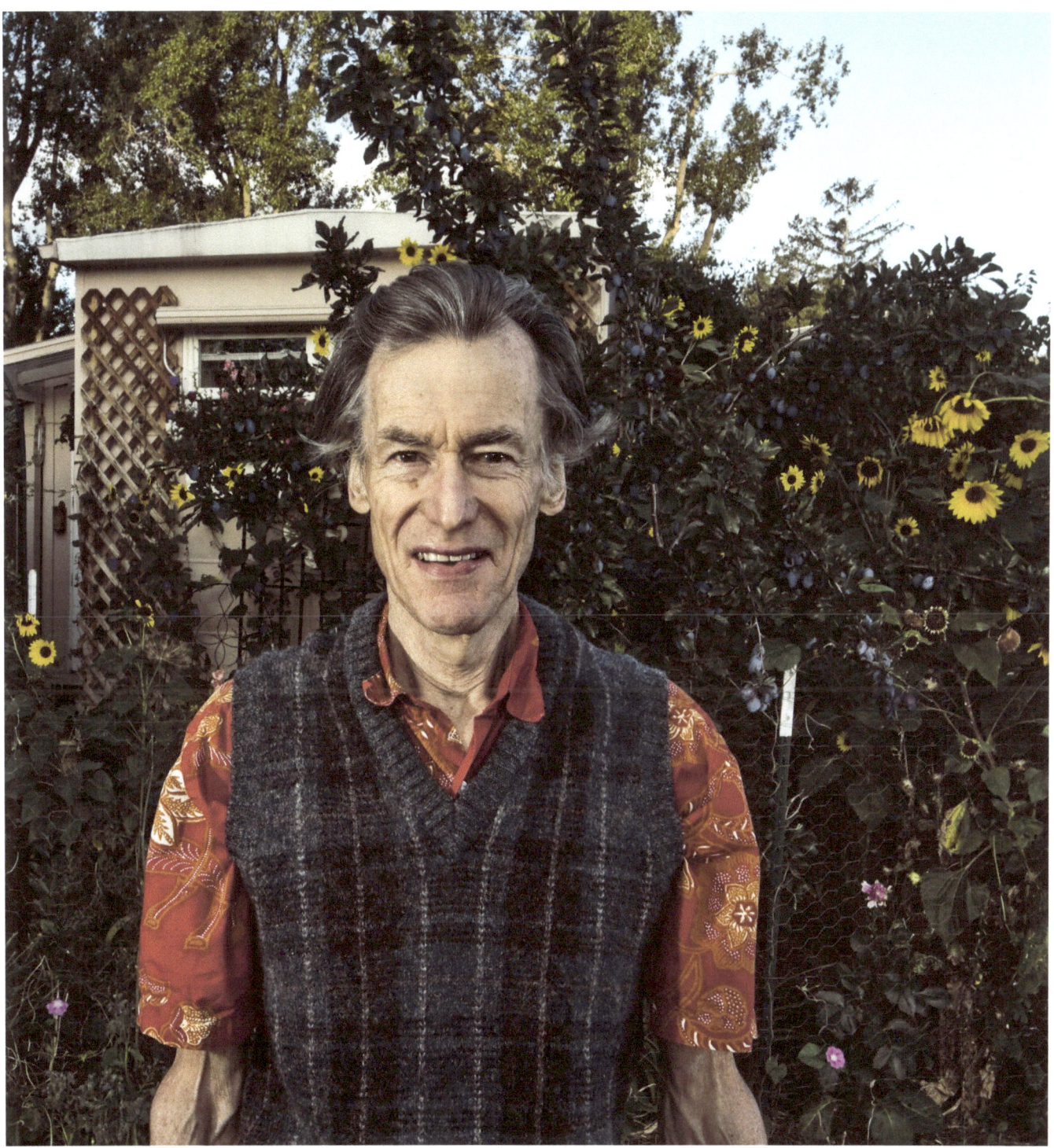

Walking my dog along the Goose Creek, that's my favorite part of living here. Watching the wildflowers change in the season. I love the proximity to the trail. I just think it's an idyllic world down there.

I have a lot more freedom here than I did living in an apartment in New York City. I don't have any dead bodies or empty bottles to step over. And Boulder is a really nice place to live. I like it.

I've lived in all different kinds of situations, in different countries. I'm surprised I ended up here. But it's a nice place to end up.

-S.

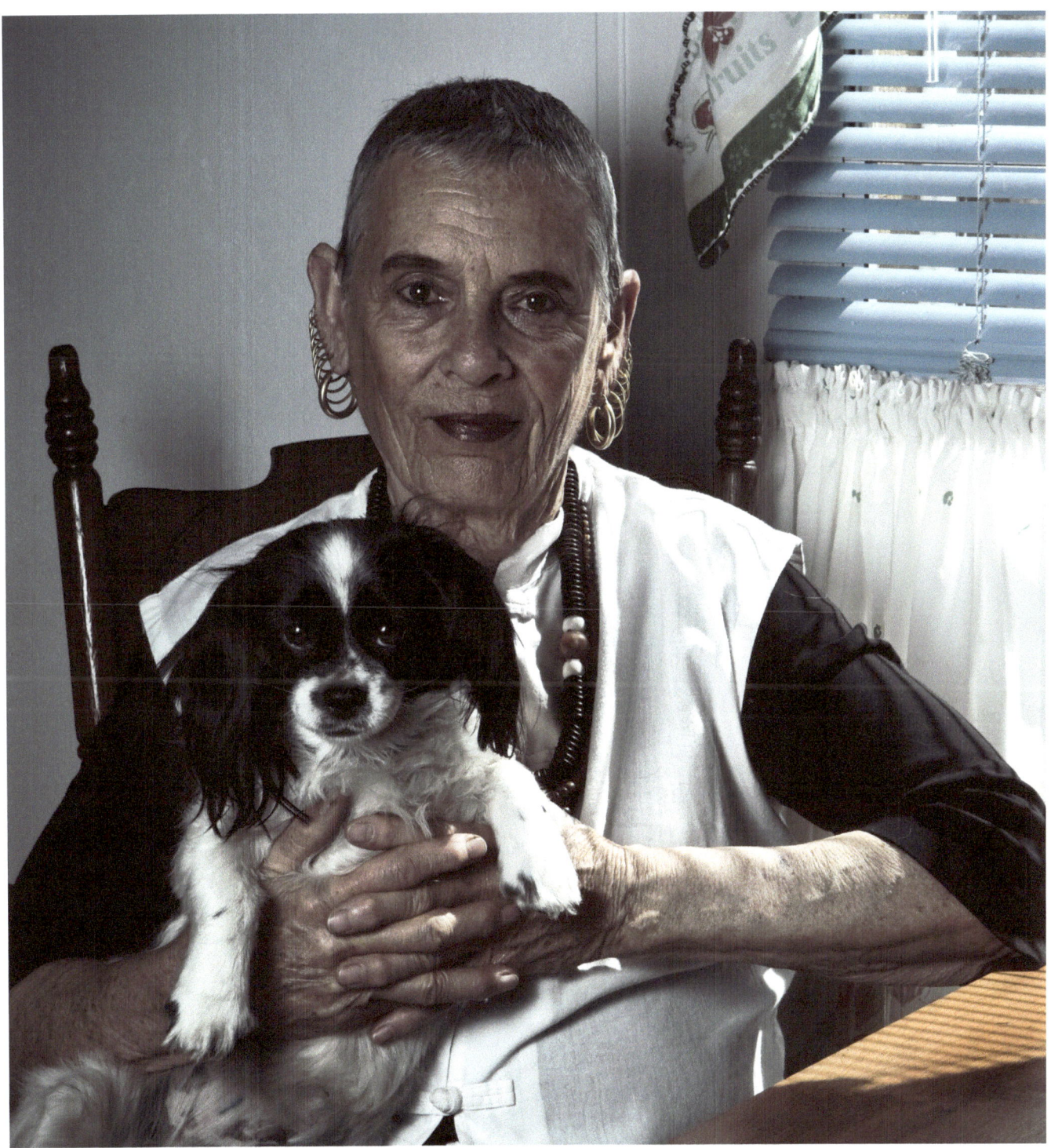

I've lived here 7 months. I have friends who have lived in this park for a while. Every time I would come visit here, I liked the feeling I got. When I separated from my husband, I wanted to move here.

This park, in particular, has a real feeling of community. All the people I've met here are really wonderful. The park, with its lower costs, also enabled me to have my own place. I don't have a huge yard, which is a plus for me, and perfect for living on my own. It's very homey and comfortable. A big "aah" comes over me when I come home. It feels very very good to me to live here.

If people have reactions to my living in a trailer park, I don't pick up on it. I don't have issues with living here.

-T.

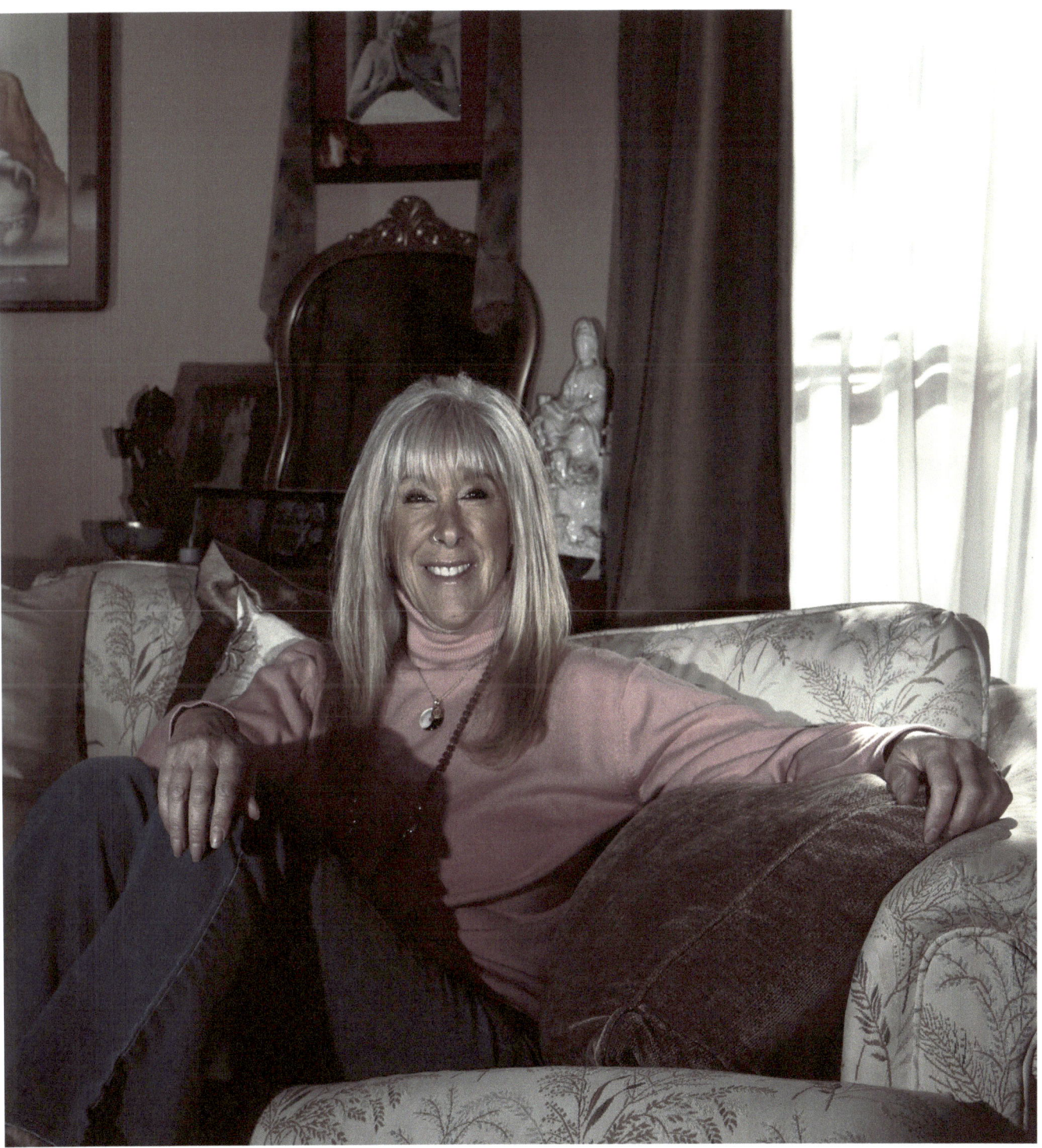

Unavailable for comment.

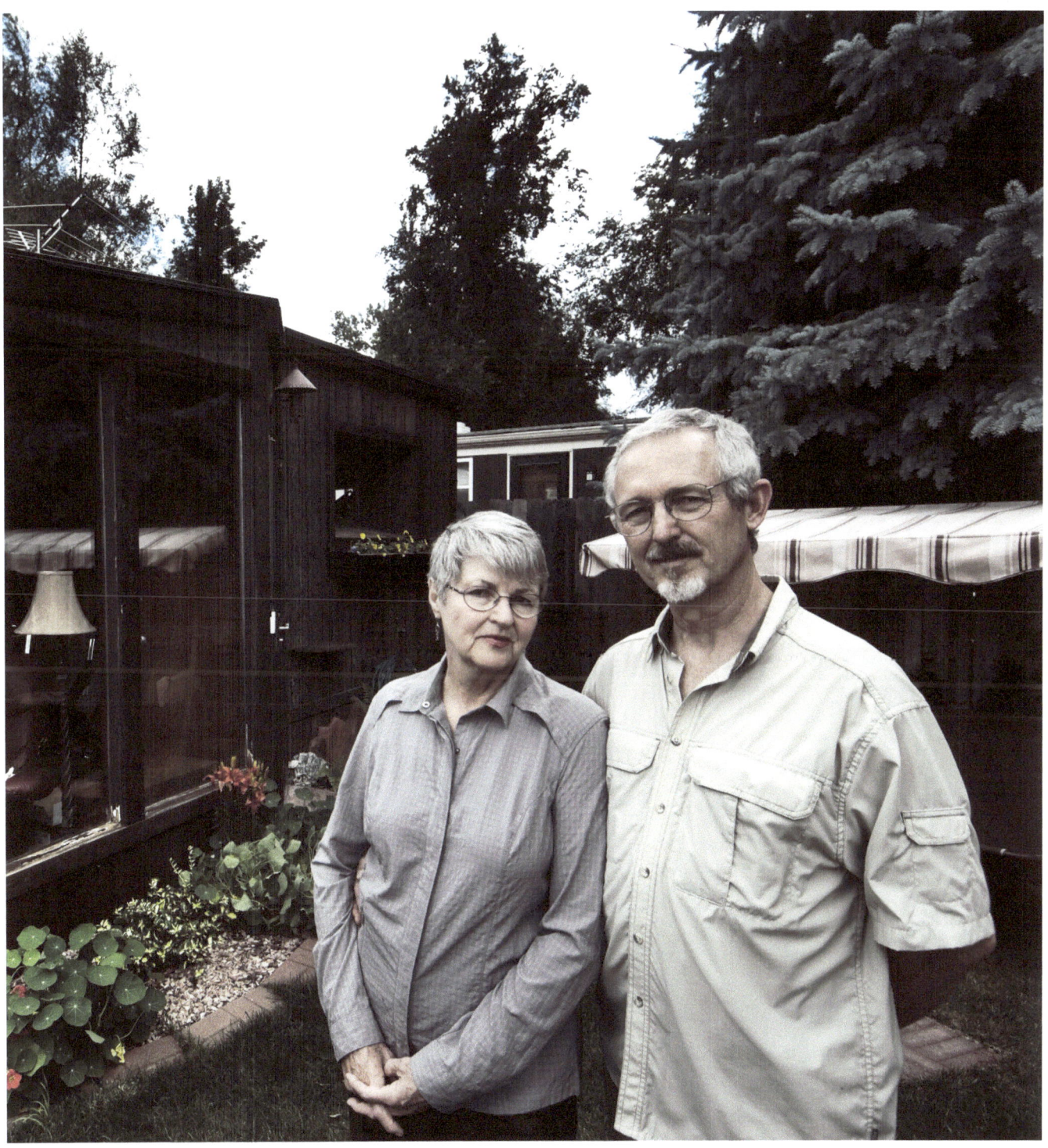

G: I was here in 1949. Canyon Boulevard was a dirt road and had railroad tracks. I watched this town grow and get set up.

We came here on a vacation (we were living in Kentucky at the time). I grew up in Boulder, but J had never been here before. We met a guy at Unity Church and who told us about this park. We didn't even know it was here!

J: We couldn't afford to live in Boulder unless we lived here. We like the location. We can walk to the YMCA and Whole Foods. We go to a lot of stuff at the university. The public library is incredible. There's always something to do.

G: I knew what the energy was like here, and I'm happy. I knew that J would be happy here.

-G & J

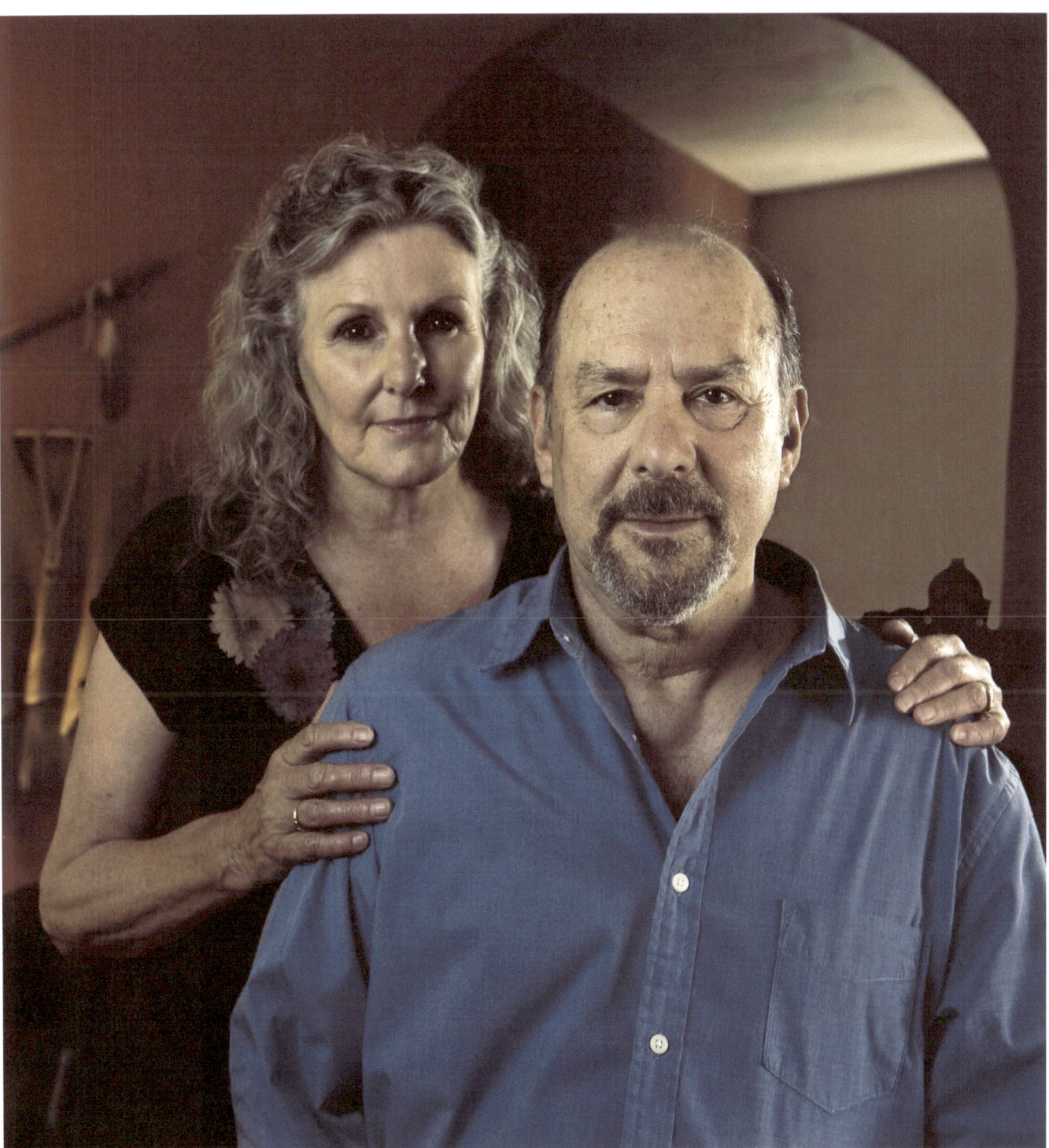

I've been here 7 years. I used to live in a different trailer in the park.

I decided to move out, but I didn't want to try and find a whole new environment. The park is in a good location and affordable. I like the sense of stability in the park, and that friends aren't far. I can ride my bike to the grocery store. There are beautiful trees. For the most part, I think it's a good place.

When I moved, I found this trailer that is basically an expanded closet, a single-wide without any insulation value and little space. I tore out the closest to have more windows. But this home was affordable, and for the price of insulating it, I might as well buy another trailer. So I've decided to make this space more aesthetically pleasing for me, even though a sunnier location and better insulation would make the biggest difference.

It seems like have been more young people wanting to live sensibly and more affordably. They want to live in Boulder, but can't afford a traditional sort of home.

Sometimes I feel a stigma for living in a trailer park. But it's in my own head.

-P.

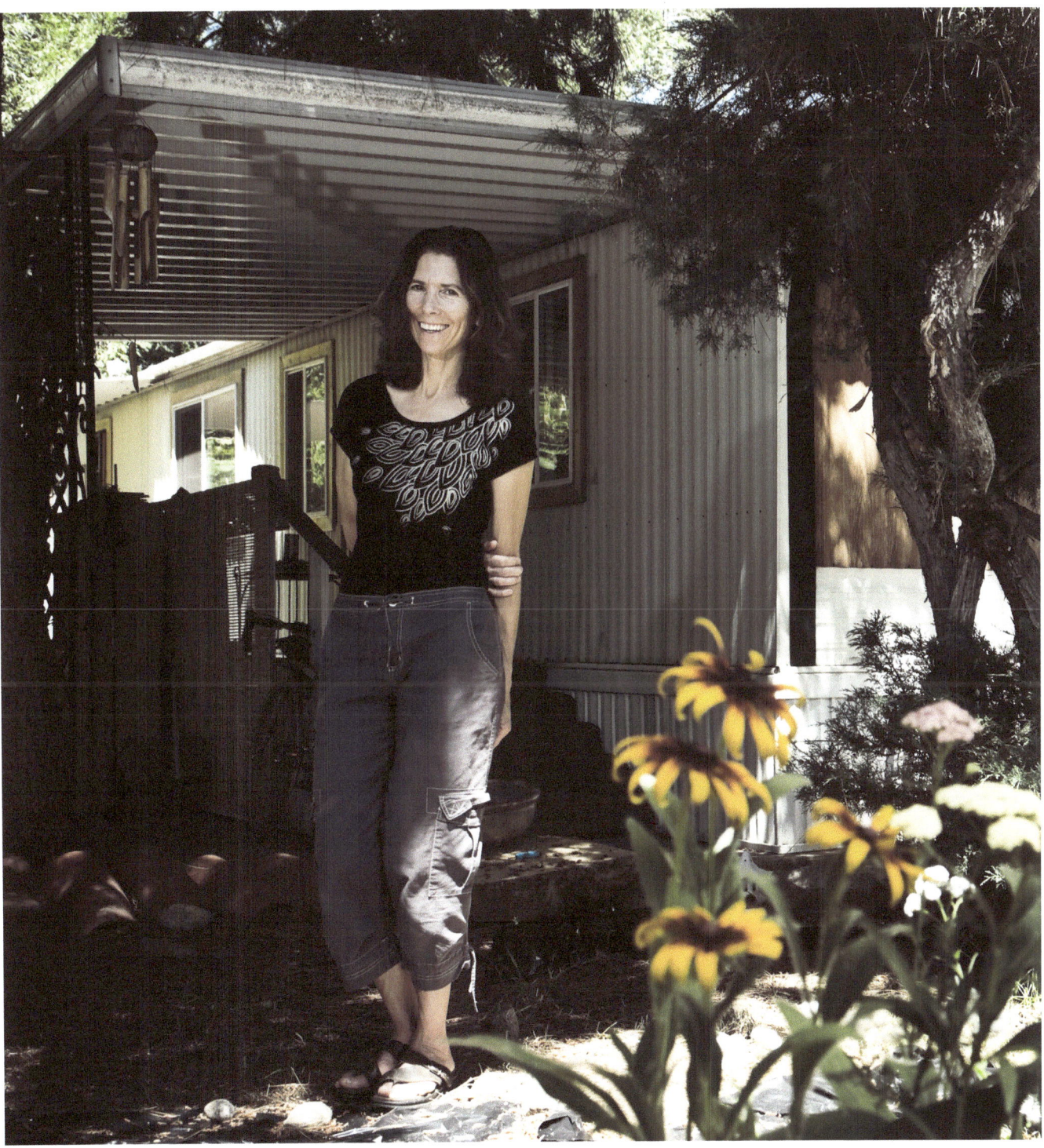

I've been in the park three years now. I'm a sophomore at CU. When I moved to Boulder, my stepfather thought I should invest in a trailer.

A lot of people laugh at the idea of living in a trailer park. I like that it's my own place and I can be my own boss. I appreciate having a garden. It's nice that the place is very private.

Nobody my age lives here. At 21, I'm the youngest person I've met here. A trailer park is little too much like a community. There are so many laws I've got to follow. I'm not really good with the community thing.

Is there any advantage? I can't be very spontaneous here because of the trailer. For example, I'm thinking of doing a year abroad, but I can't do it because it's too much. I can't rent out the trailer, and it would take about a year to sell it.

I've never lived in a condo or in an apartment with other people. I know I'd hate it, but I'd still like to try it.

-K.

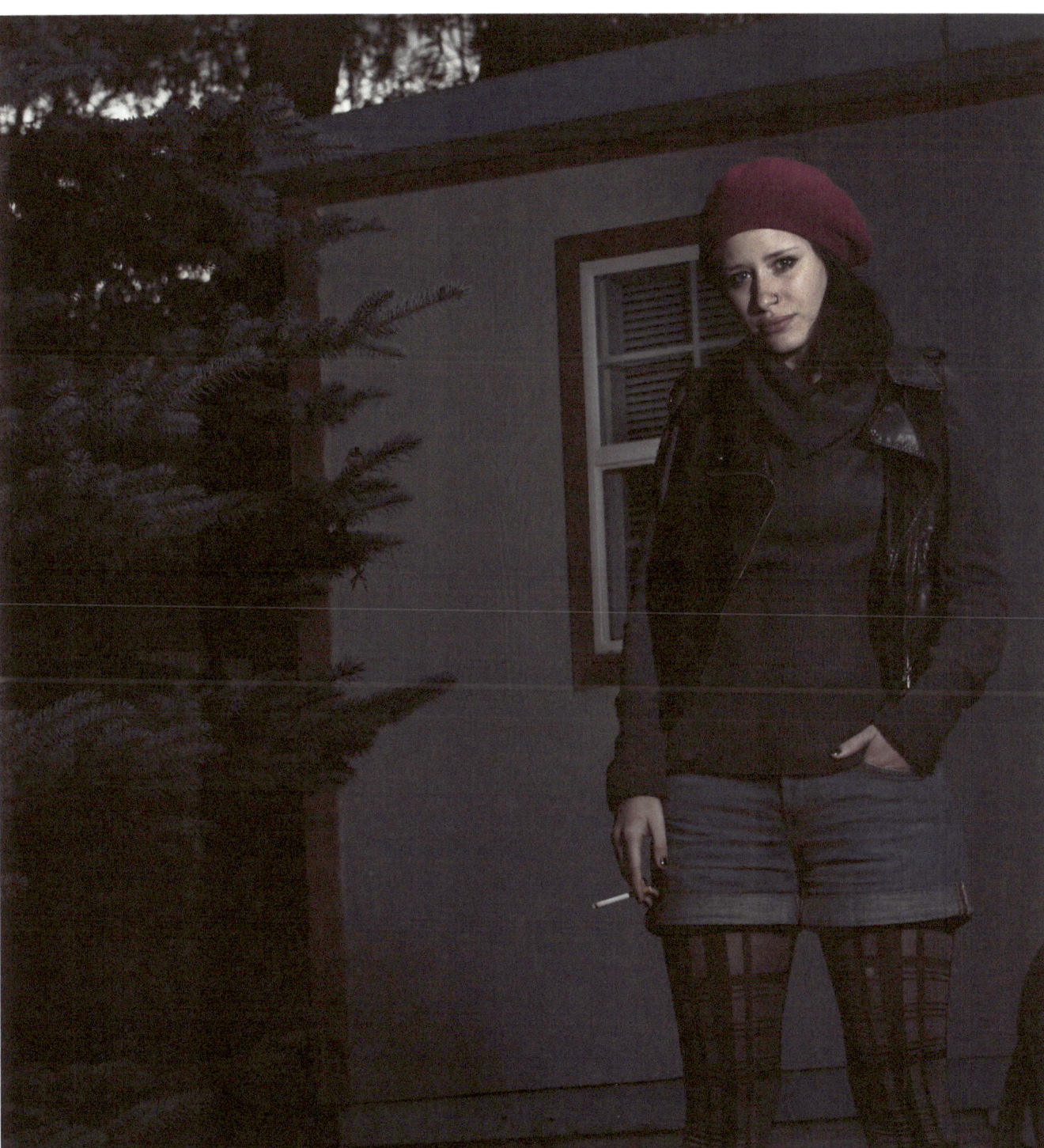

S: I'm not American, and it's been a huge transition for me to live in a trailer park. In Australia, where I'm from, you take vacations in trailers. You don't live in them.

I met F when I moved to Boulder. When I first saw F's place, I was shocked. I thought, F lives here? Despite my problems with the way the trailer looked, my body was very relaxed. It was very still here, with a lot of trees.

Four months later, we got married in the trailer. I was living in an apartment up on Pine Street before the marriage, but I was more at home in this funny little trailer. I moved out of the apartment, sold my house in Australia, downsized, and moved into the trailer.

It's been hard for me, and it's been wonderful. This is where love found me. And love is not about appearances and a beautiful home. I knew this love between us was very real, so I basically gave everything to that.

F: I like what renovating our trailer has brought out of me. I get work done, then basically sit back and enjoy it in a very empty-minded way. It's been a real purification process, it's like building new ground. And it's still simple and affordable.

S: Not just in America, but all over the world, the message is that less is more. Would I want more space? Sure. But for now, this is simply right. This is where life brought me and love found me. It's been a huge journey.

-F & S

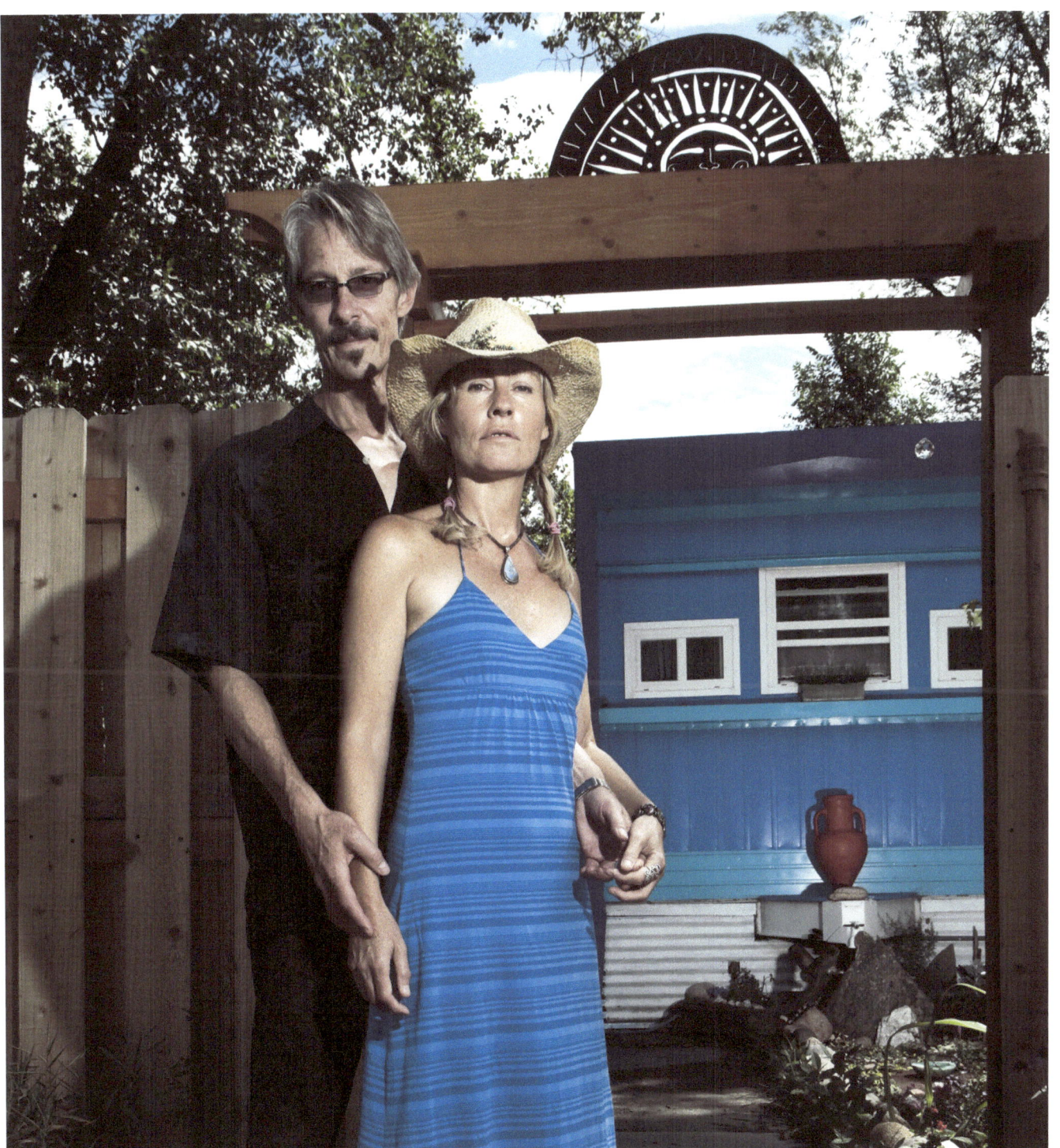

I've been here six years. I was initially drawn to the fact that a close group of residents were helping make this park happen, going through the process of building it up together and celebrating success as a group. I was also attracted to the inexpensive living here, especially considering how unstable the world is today.

I have experienced a lot of appreciation from people for what a great place this park is to live. Many people like the quality of the homes here, the funky vibe, the way it's surrounded by trees. They can be envious when they hear about how inexpensive it is to live here.

From a more unconscious place, I have perceived judgment leaking out that reflects the American cultural view of mobile home and trailer living, that's it's for lower-class people, white trash and the like. That judgment shows up from time to time amongst the people living here. I have even found it in my own mind. It's a more subtle kind of judgment, though, and doesn't usually come from a conscious or intentional place.

-R.

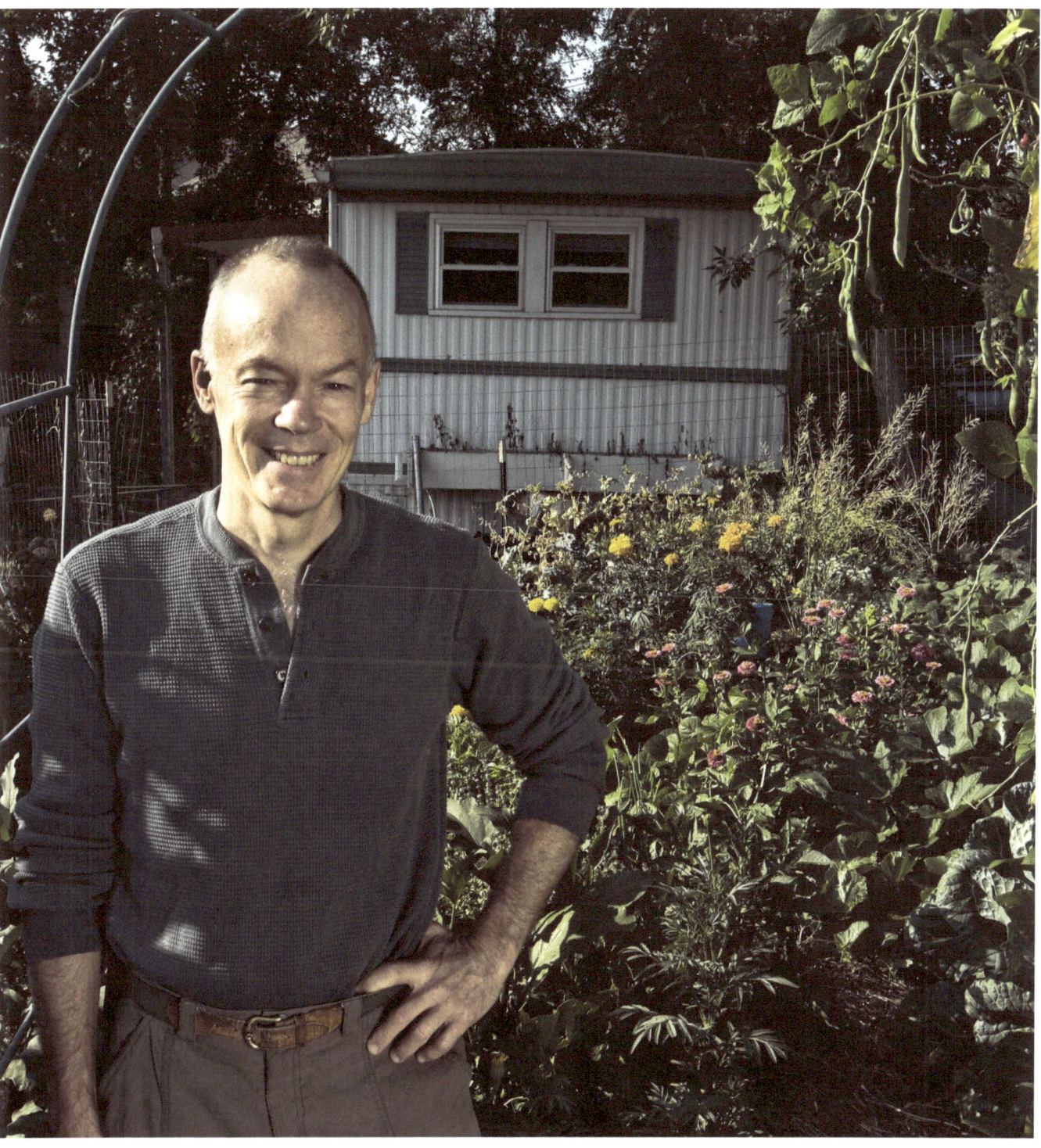

Unavailable for comment.

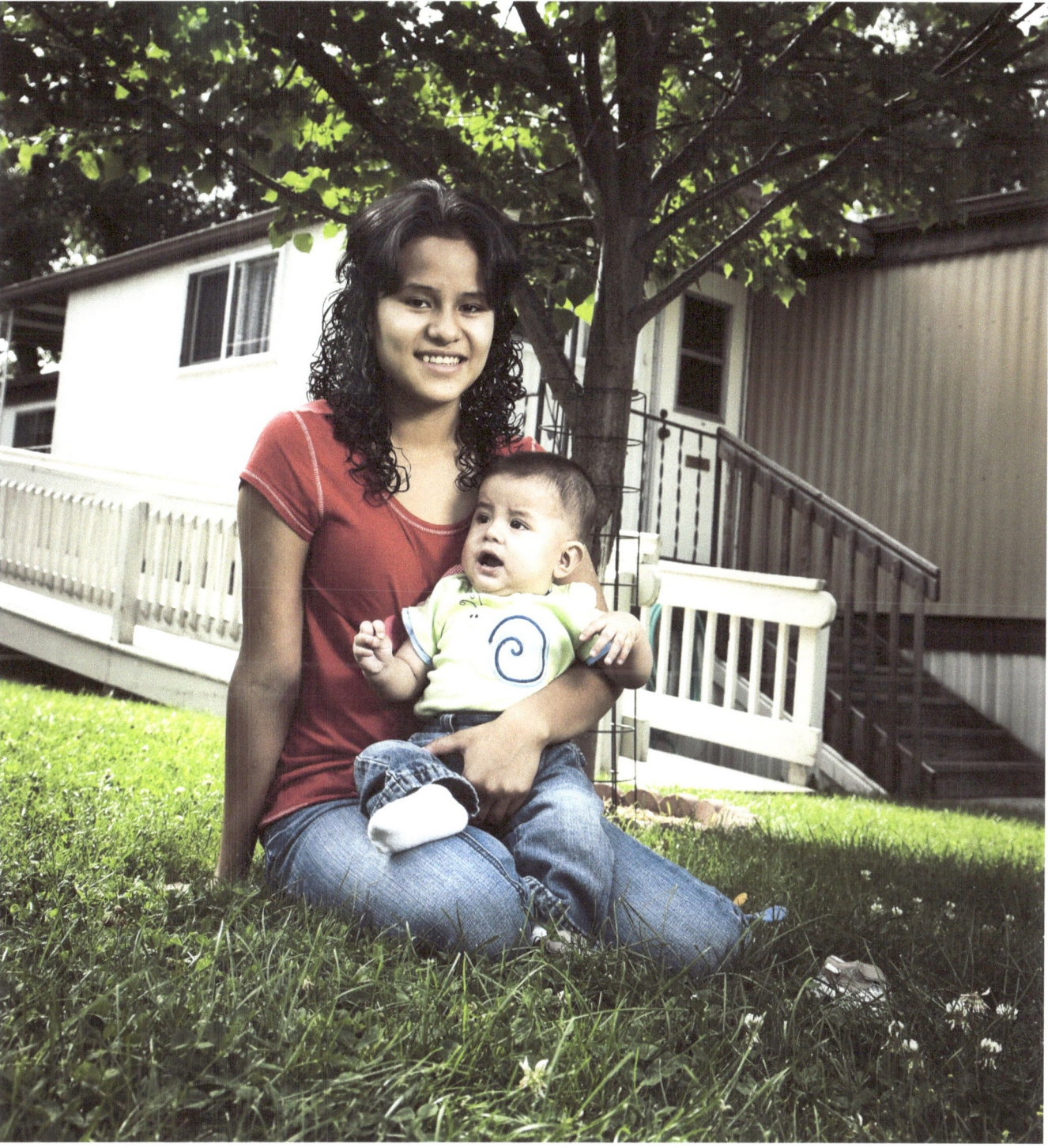

I've lived here in the park just over 6 years now. I love it.

When I started looking for a place of my own, I quickly realized that I couldn't afford to rent even an apartment here any more, unless I was willing to live in a shoebox.

These places here are great! We have our own home, with space around each of them, all within a nice little community, which is right in the middle of town.

And I guess that's my favorite part of living here. My own place, no shared walls, space for a garden, right in the heart of Boulder, Colorado. And it's affordable! I like that too.

When people hear for the first time that I live in a trailer park, I often think I see this look pass over them. These questions they might have. Like, I wonder how funky that is?! And when they come to visit, they are very pleasantly surprised. That's fun. Surprising people.

-S.

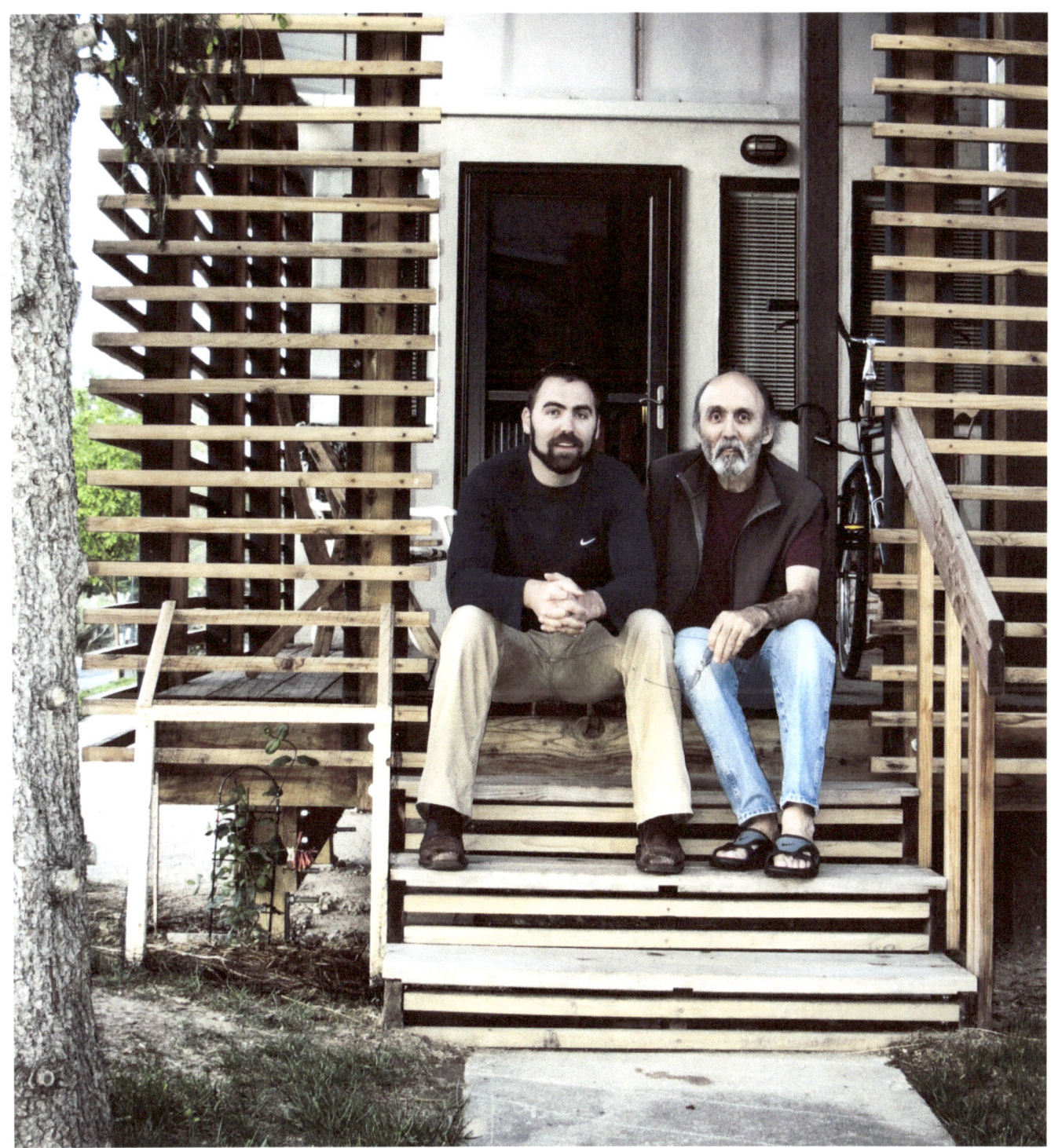

This is the first time I've lived in a trailer park. My job before I moved here was low-income weatherization. I worked on a lot of trailers in Boulder County. I realized I wanted to live in a trailer, and I really liked the Mapleton park. I like being able to afford a place that I can call my own. I have no complaints about this place, other than the fact that there are no good bus lines nearby.

With some people, when I tell them where I live, it's a conversation stopper. I think some people assume it's like living in an RV, or it's really rustic, but that's not the right assumption. More often than not, I find people are interested in this place. They bike through here and think it's really cool that I live here.

-J

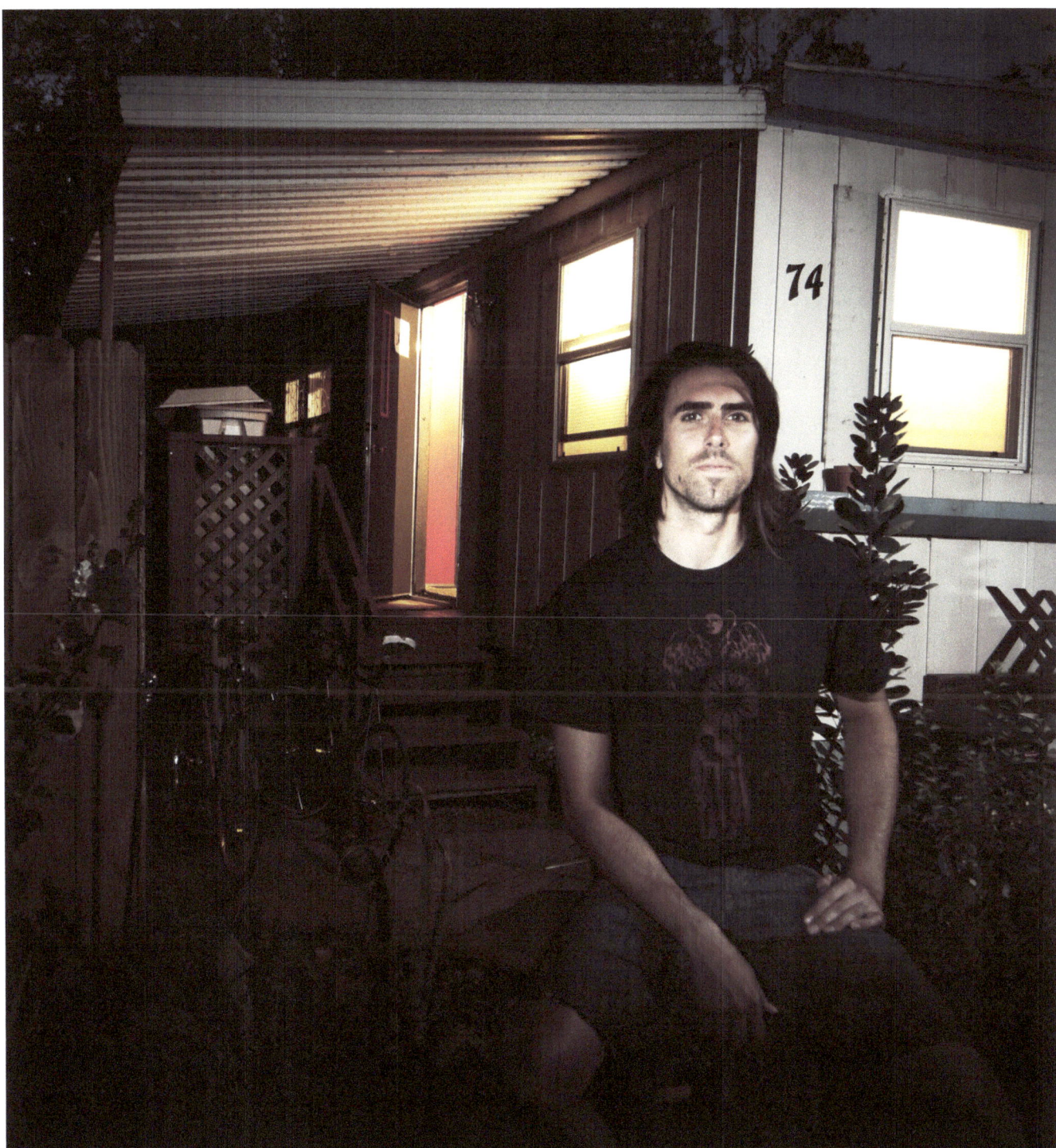

I used to kind of snub my nose at trailer parks. Until I lived in Florida. There, they had a large trailer park and it was prime property. A developer ended up buying out lots for millions of dollars to build a luxury condo complex. Then, I thought oh! Trailer park! What a great idea!

I knew I was getting older and wouldn't be able to work all my life. I still had some big hesitations about living in a trailer, but this (double-wide home) was custom built. It is so beautiful. And the park is so diverse. Everything is in here. I like the accepting of people who aren't ordinary.

Lots of people here seem to be taking pride in their places, fixing them up. Some of the trailers are still pretty bad, but you can always gut the inside and transform it.

I feel so grateful to be trailer trash. I like it. It allows all sorts of things--like affording to live here in the center of Boulder.

-S

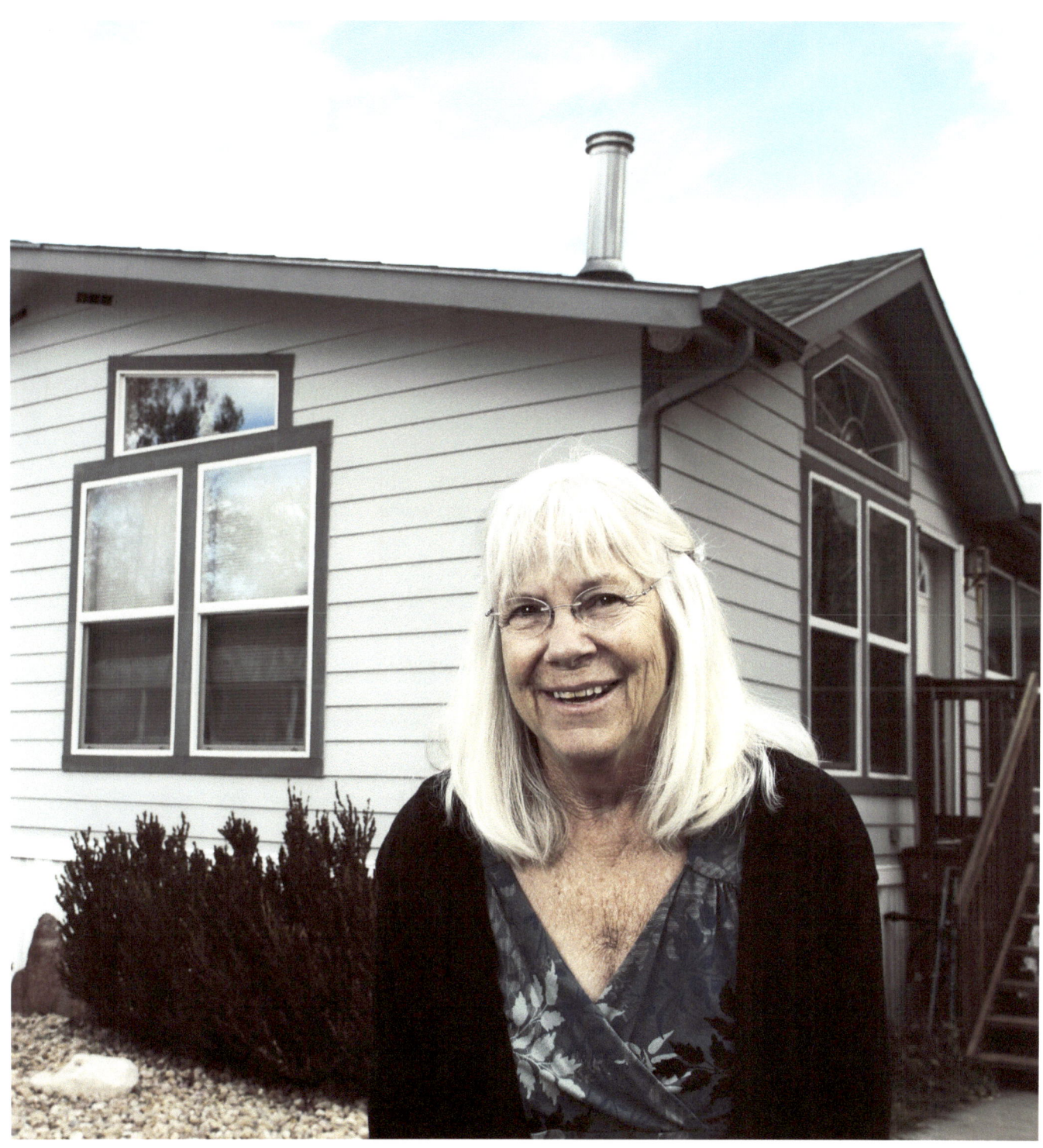

We've lived here 10 or 11 years. We like living here. It's very calm. There's no violence or crime. There are nice people here; we have good friendships with the neighbors.

I like living in a mobile home because it's independent. In apartments, we can't live here because if the kids jump the neighbors will complain.

The only downside is that the family is growing. Sometimes the trailer is too small, so some of the family have to go live somewhere else.

-J

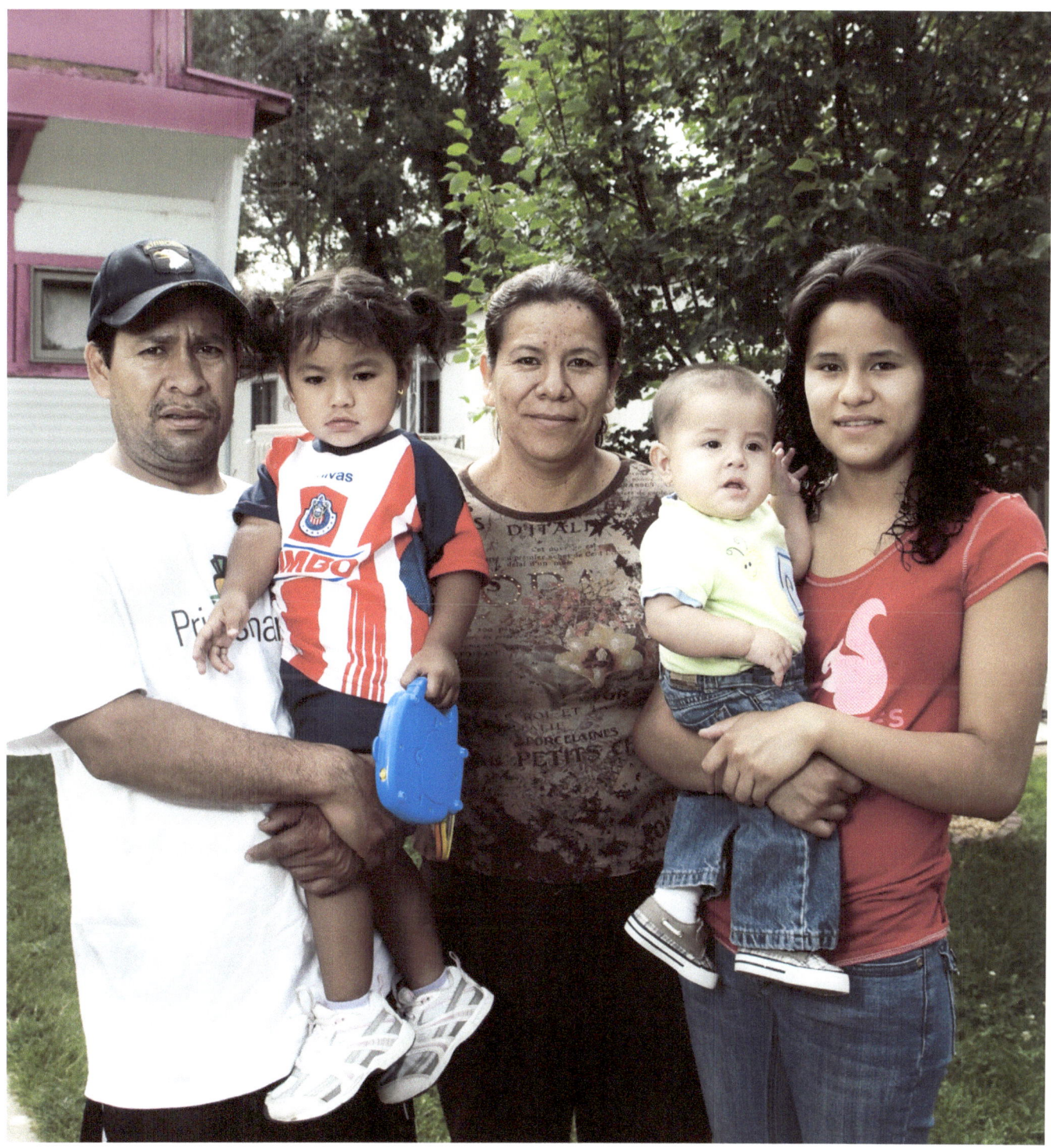

Unavailable for comment.

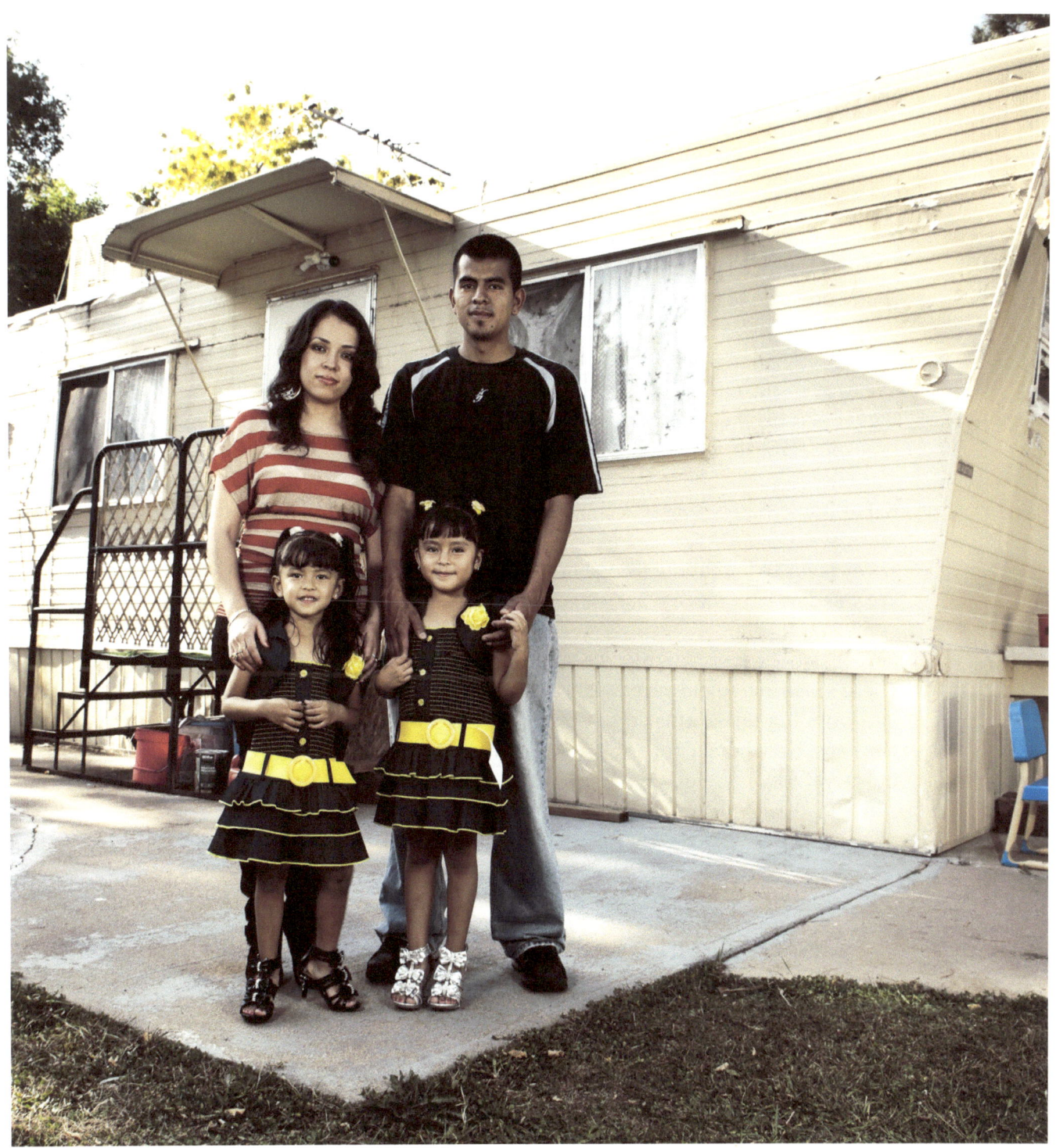

H: There's a lot of judgment about trailer trash. It's kind of like you can live on the wrong side of the tracks. Minds are capable of all sorts of things. Why bother to react?

I've lived in big houses, owned big houses. But there's too much upkeep. Bigger places take so much more energy. It's also safe here. You don't hear of break-ins. I mean, who would want to break into a trailer?

K: For Boulder, this is a great choice. Waterfront property right in Boulder.

H: My favorite part about living here is that it's inexpensive. We have a nice space. We can do pretty much what we want with it and not worry about big property taxes.

There's also incredible potential in a community like this. People can cooperate and work together. I think there are already community gardens, orchards, chickens, bees here. There's all kinds of potential that we haven't been able to utilize yet. But hopefully in the future...

-K & H

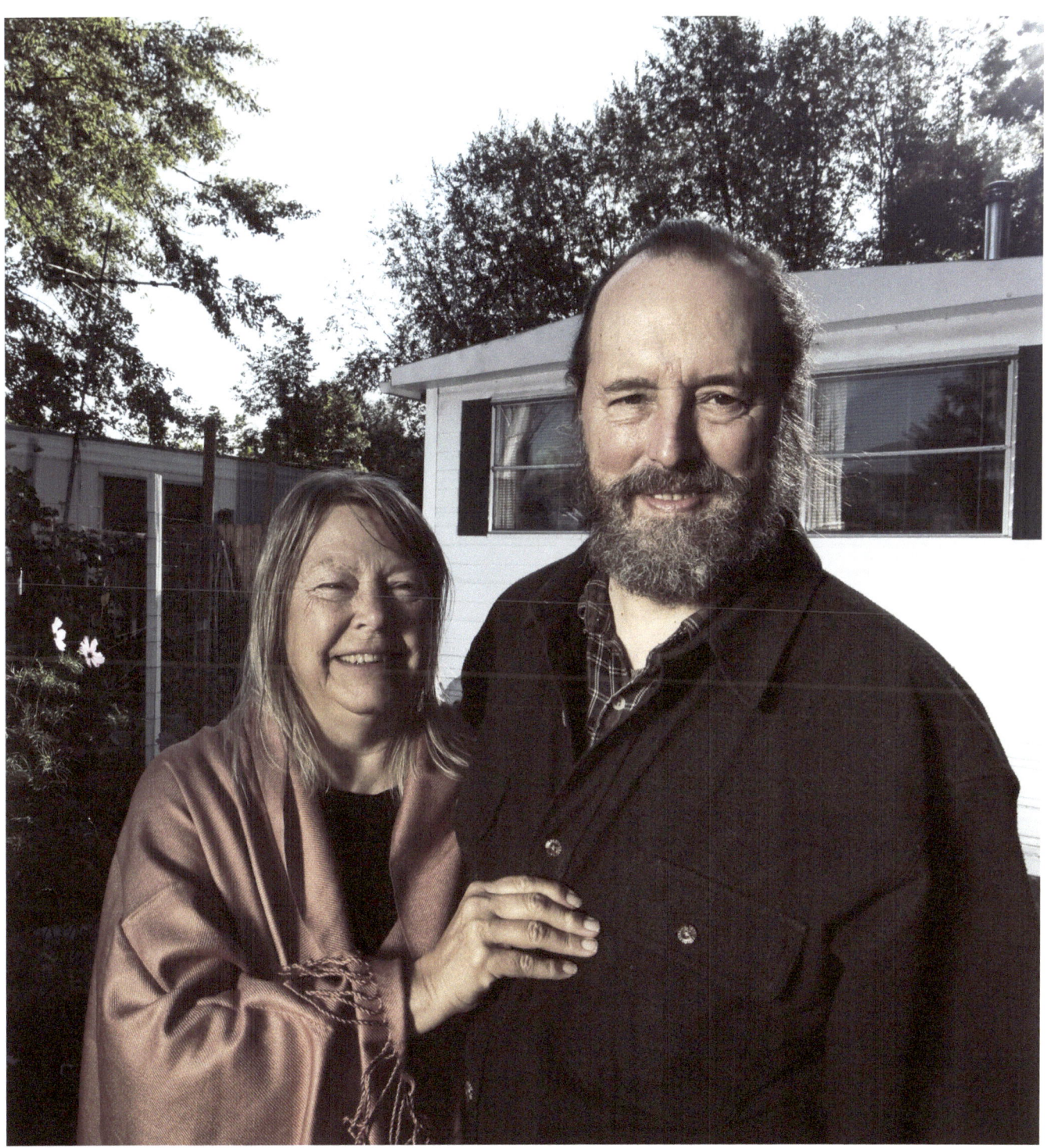

This park is a little gem inside of a very expensive town. There's a great opportunity to take this little box you live in and create something special. It's really cool what people have done with their homes. I like the simplicity aspect of living in a small space, too. I don't have to be concerned about making a ton of money. I can ride my bike downtown.

In terms of people judging the park, I've noticed it's not so much what they say, but the look on their face, like they're trying to hide their reaction. Talking about living here begins to break down their stereotypes. I see people opening up more with the discussion. And I see it as an opportunity to let go of my own judgments about living in a mobile home park.

-K.

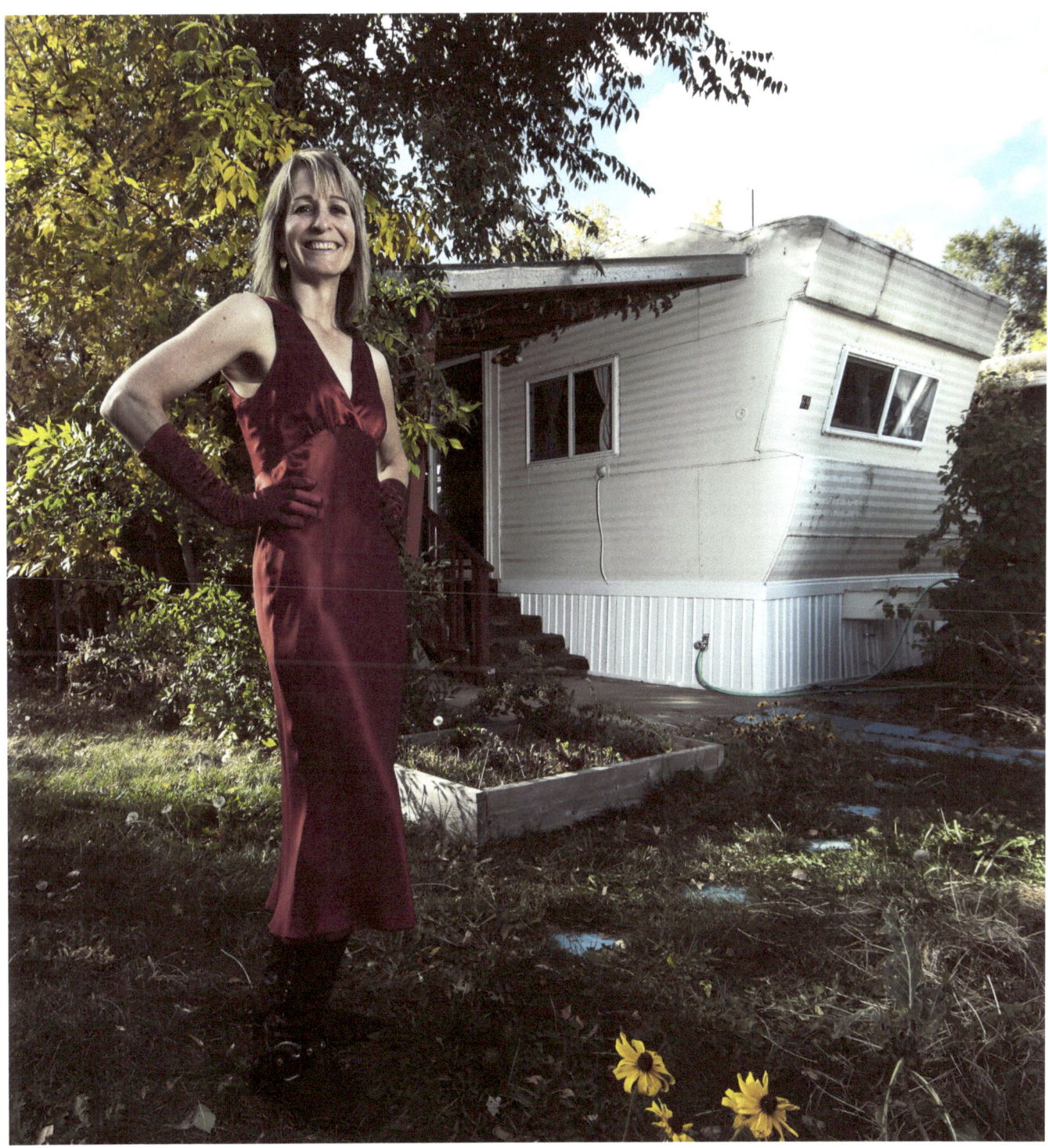

I looked at several different condos and townhomes before buying this place. With them, you have to pay a monthly homeowners' association fee, and that's very expensive. Here, for $25,000, I made this place exactly the way I wanted it.

When I moved, even my friends judged me for moving from a house into a mobile home park. It's a stereotype people have because they don't know what you can do with your mobile home.

The park has a very nice sense of being in a community, not like in a bunch of apartment buildings. We are close together, but we don't share walls, and we have our own little yards.

I wish people could see what you can do with a mobile home. You don't have to spend hundreds of thousands of dollars having a beautiful home.

-S.

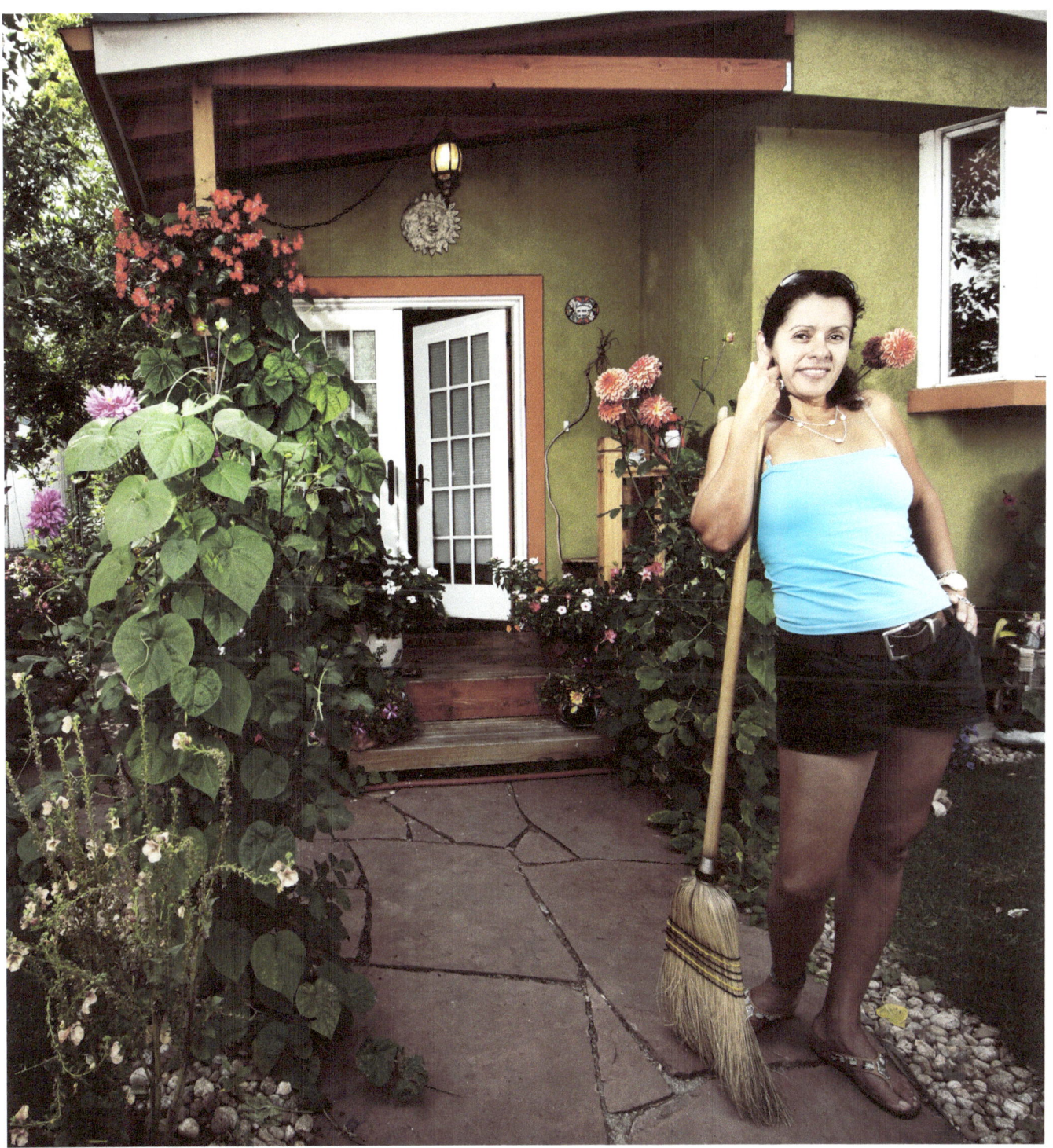

When I was younger, "The Big Orange Splot" by D. Manus Pinkwater was my favorite book. In it, a seagull flies over Mr. Plumbean's house with a bucket of paint and leaves a big orange spot on his roof. At first Mr. Plumbean thinks it's a stain, but it actually leads him to build his dream home in a neighborhood where everything looked the same. One by one, people followed his example and built their own dream homes. There's a unique charm at the Mapleton park that reminds me of that story.

People have this stereotype of what a trailer park is, with the poverty and all that. There's also something beyond that, where people choose to live more sustainably and affordably. Half of the people in this park are extremely well educated people who choose to live like this. Here, they can be energy efficient, they have a small, simple home and don't have to spend all their money on housing.

I'd say a quarter of the people who live here leave for a month out of the year, for places like India and Mexico, where they can travel and experience the cultures they love. Living here, you can afford to do that.

Over the years, I've had to work with how I say that I live in a trailer park, my own pride and fear of reaction from people. I've learned that once you become comfortable with it yourself, it helps dissipate other peoples' misinformation.

-L.

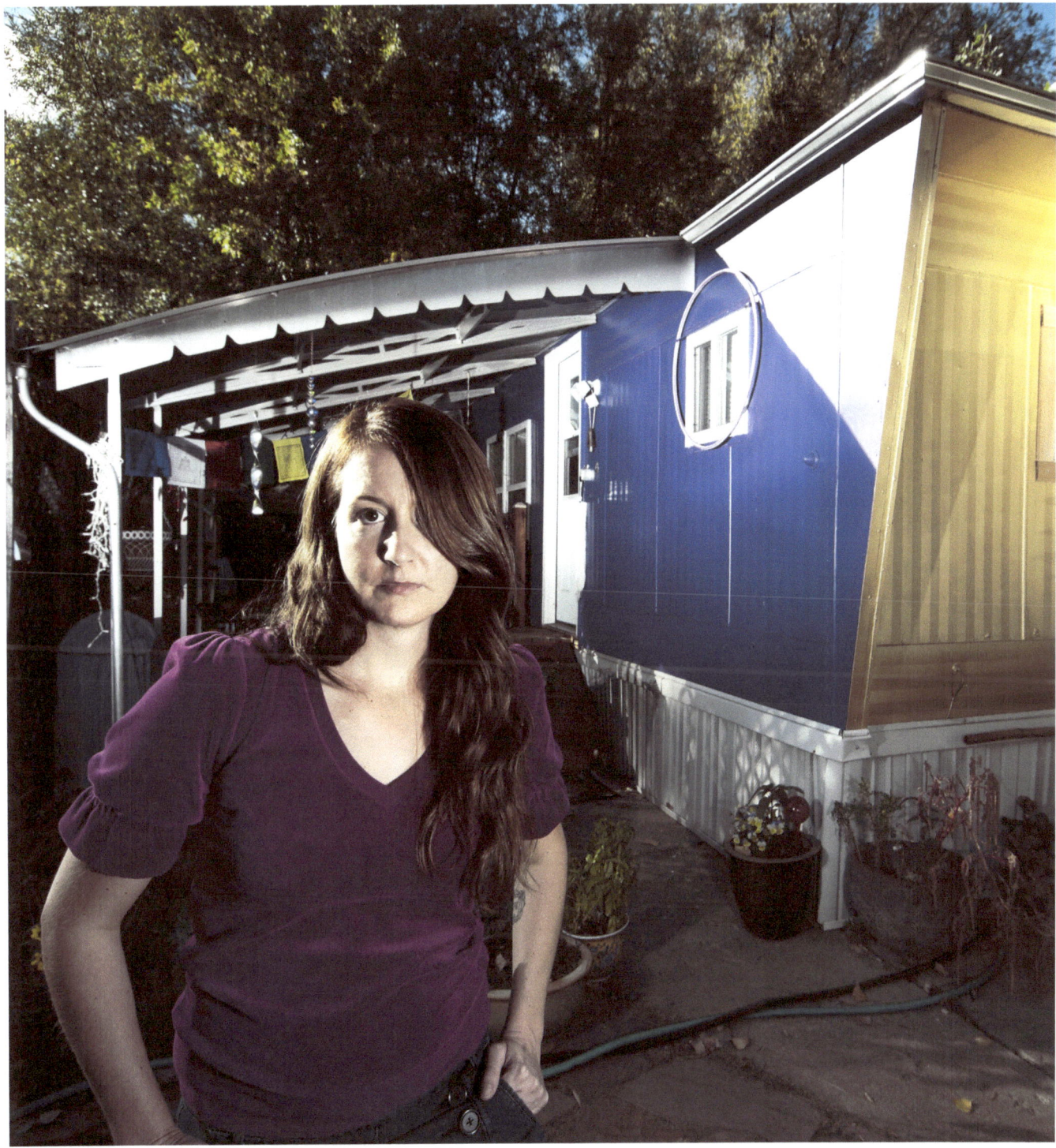

I've lived in the park about 2 and a half years now.

And, I've always been fascinated with mobile homes and small homes.

My favorite part of living in the park is good neighbors and everyone knows each other.

Privacy can be hard to come by.

-M.

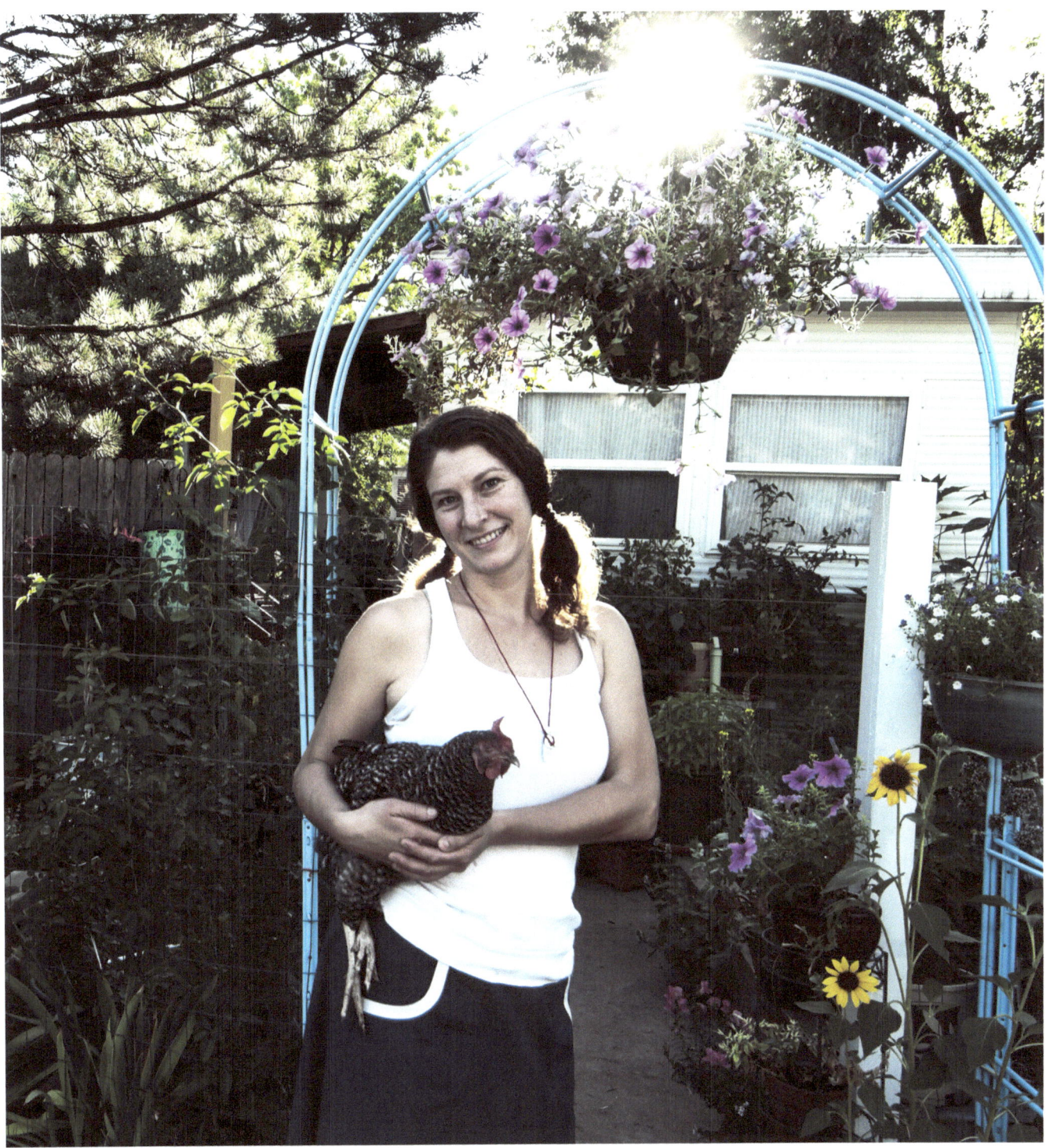

Unavailable for comment.

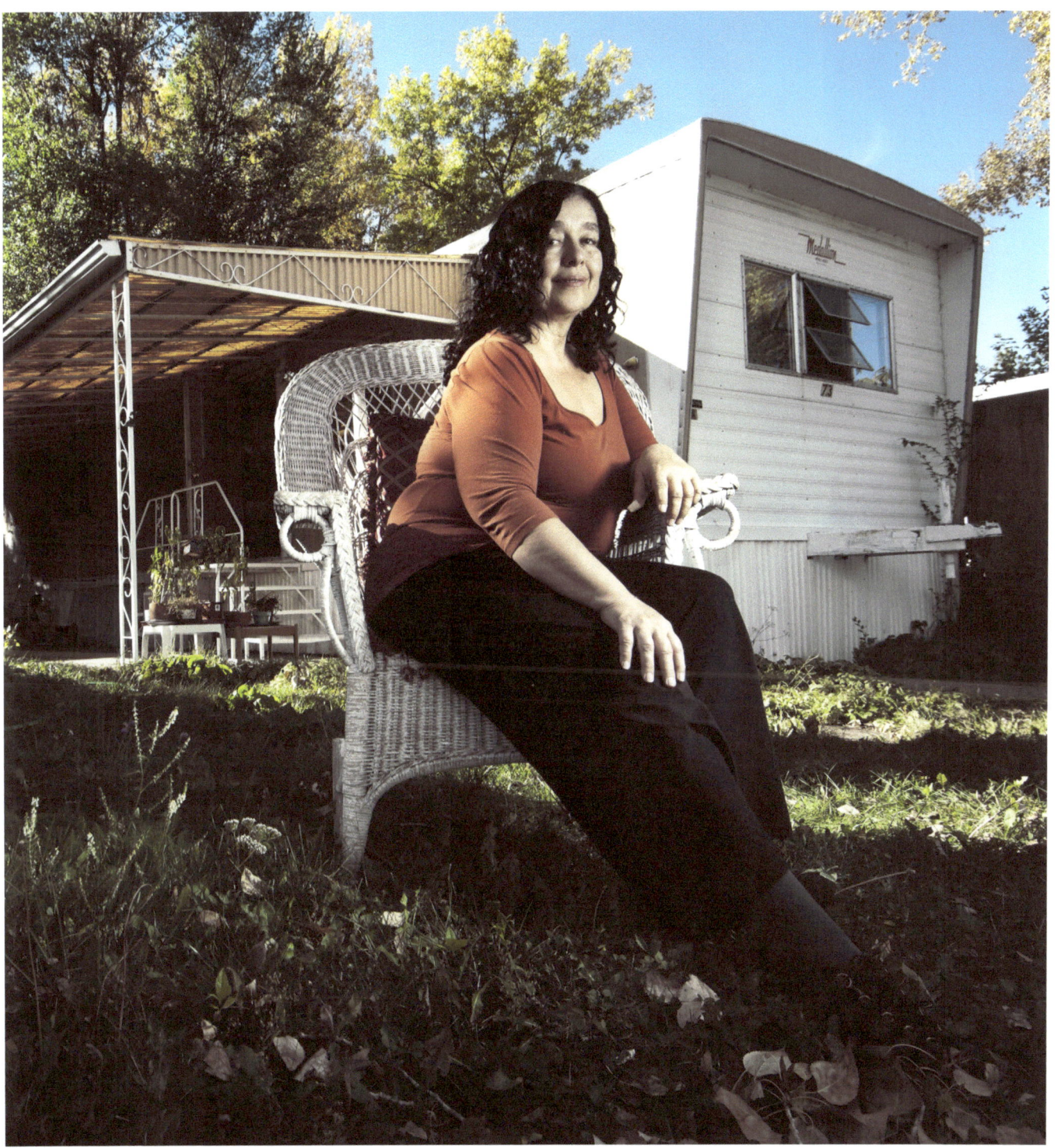

I'm a Boulder native. I was born on Mapleton, I live on Mapleton, and I work on Mapleton. I've been here at the park for 32 years. It's amazing how many people I've known who have had to move out of Boulder, because they can't afford it anymore.

This trailer has been a great place to live and heal. It's just the right size for one person. It's a small town in a small city. There's lots of diversity and uniqueness here, lots of people who are into green living. Trailer park people are normal people.

Once in a while, when people learn I live here, they give me a quizzical look. You don't think of Boulder as having mobile homes. It's nice to be able to still live here in Boulder, for a halfway affordable rent.

-L.

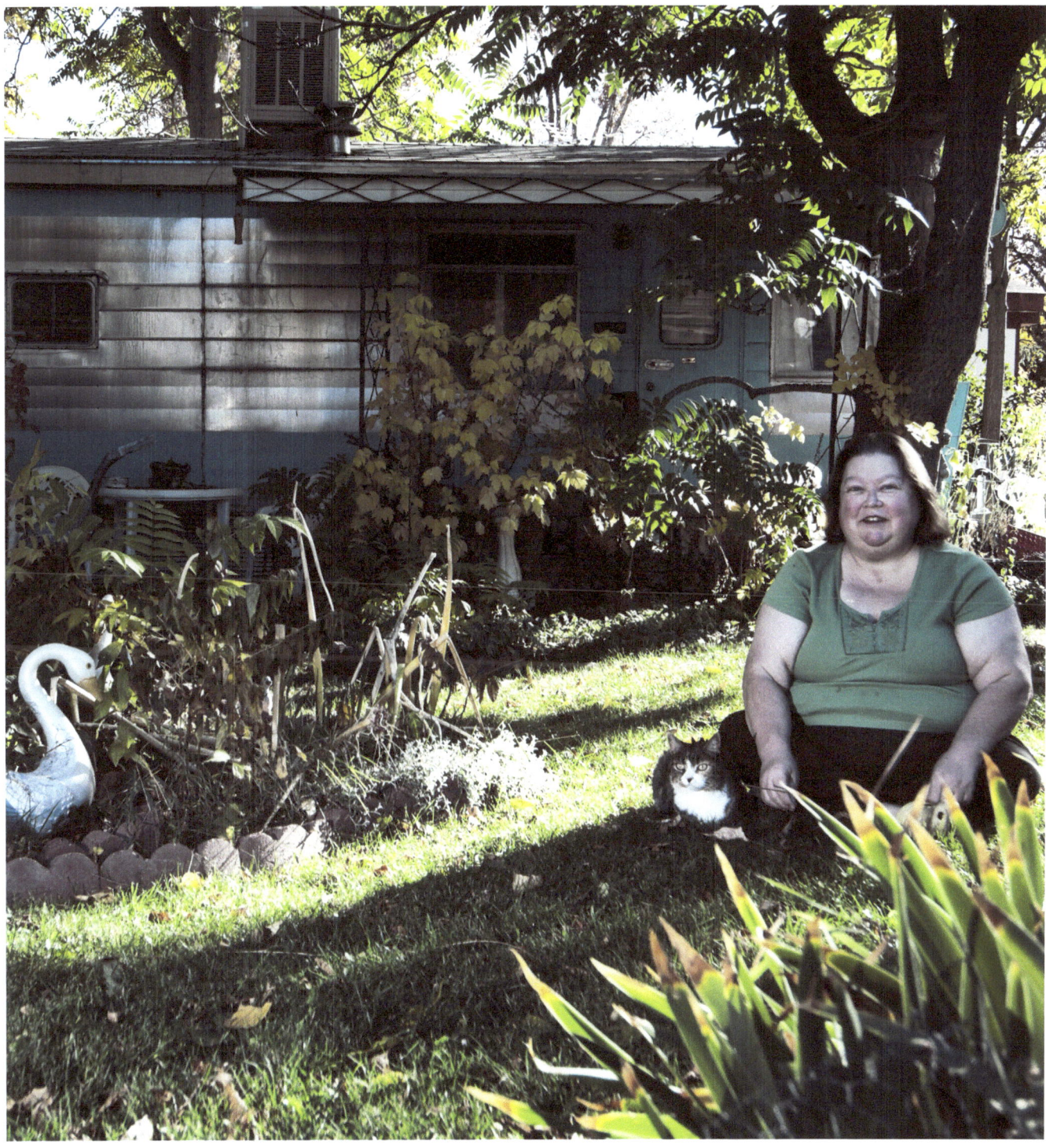

I like the trailer. It's comfortable, it fits me, it's not too big and it's not too small. Everything is walkable. There are two health food stores and a bookstore nearby, I can easily walk downtown, and the bike path is at the end of the street. I like having the ability to do things other than sink my every dime into rent or a mortgage.

What I don't like is there are a lot of attitudes about people who live in mobile homes. I used to live in a mobile home park on Valmont, with my three kids. There are a lot of trust funders and wealthy kids here in Boulder, and my kids never invited kids from outside the neighborhood to our house. It was a loss to me that they would never tell their friends where they lived or bring them home.

Everyone is entitled to their opinion, but there was no place I could have lived in Boulder with three kids for $350 per month. Our culture is just so immersed in appearances.

-J.

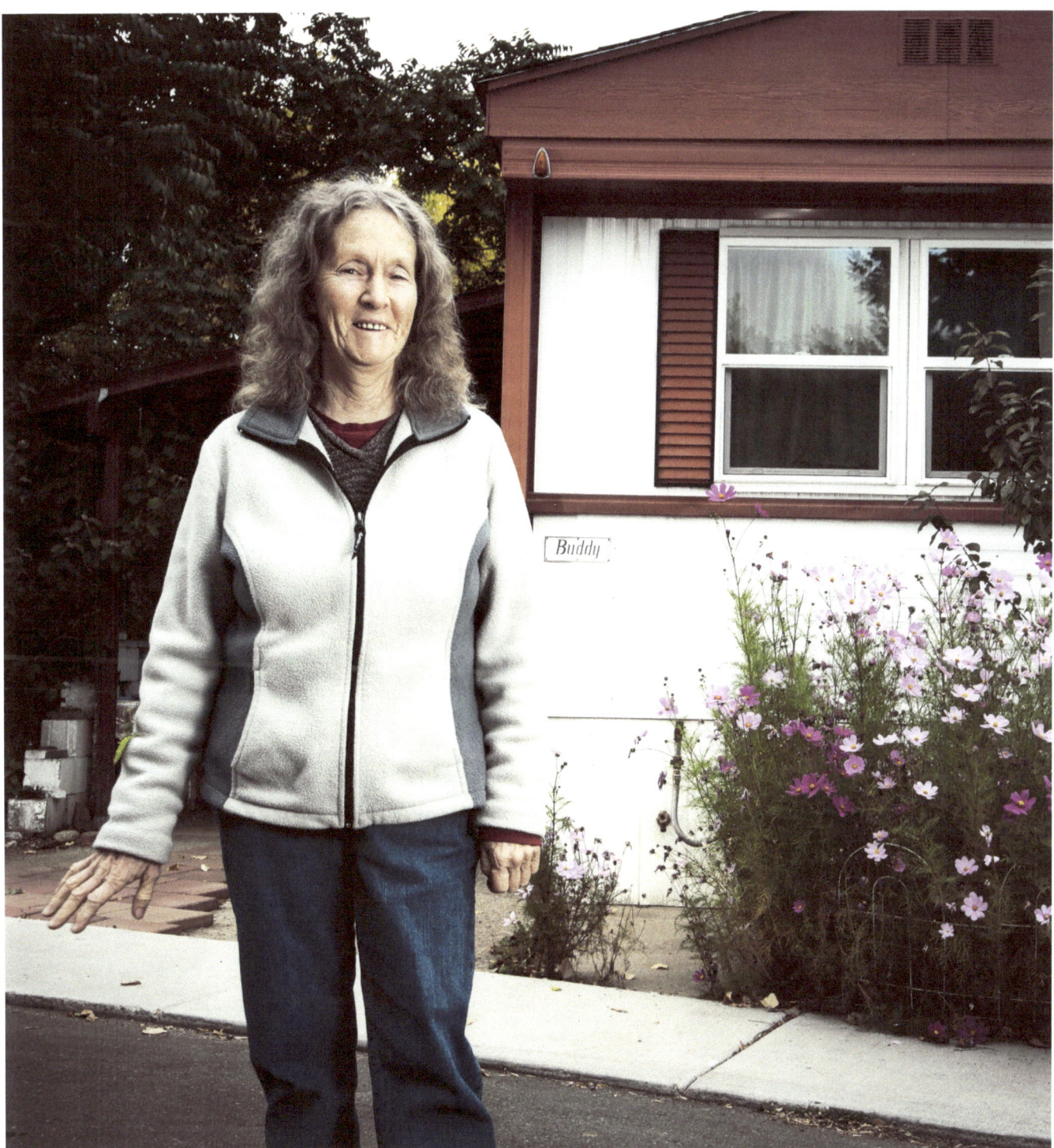

I've lived in the park for a little over six years.

What brought me here was the opportunity to own my own, affordable, home in Boulder.

My favorite part of living in the park is the sense of being in a neighborhood within a neighborhood, like we're a distinct environment, or island, within the larger and more anonymous surrounding streets of a town.

My home, though beloved, is very small to meet all of my needs, eg for having enough space to make my art in.

I've never experienced any judgment about living in the park. But then if someone I don't know well asks me where I live, I sometimes, for the hell of it, say "oh, right in the middle of Boulder," and they look at me like I must be a millionaire. ...Mostly I say in the Mapleton Mobile Home Park and they almost invariably tell me how many people they know that also live here!

-R.

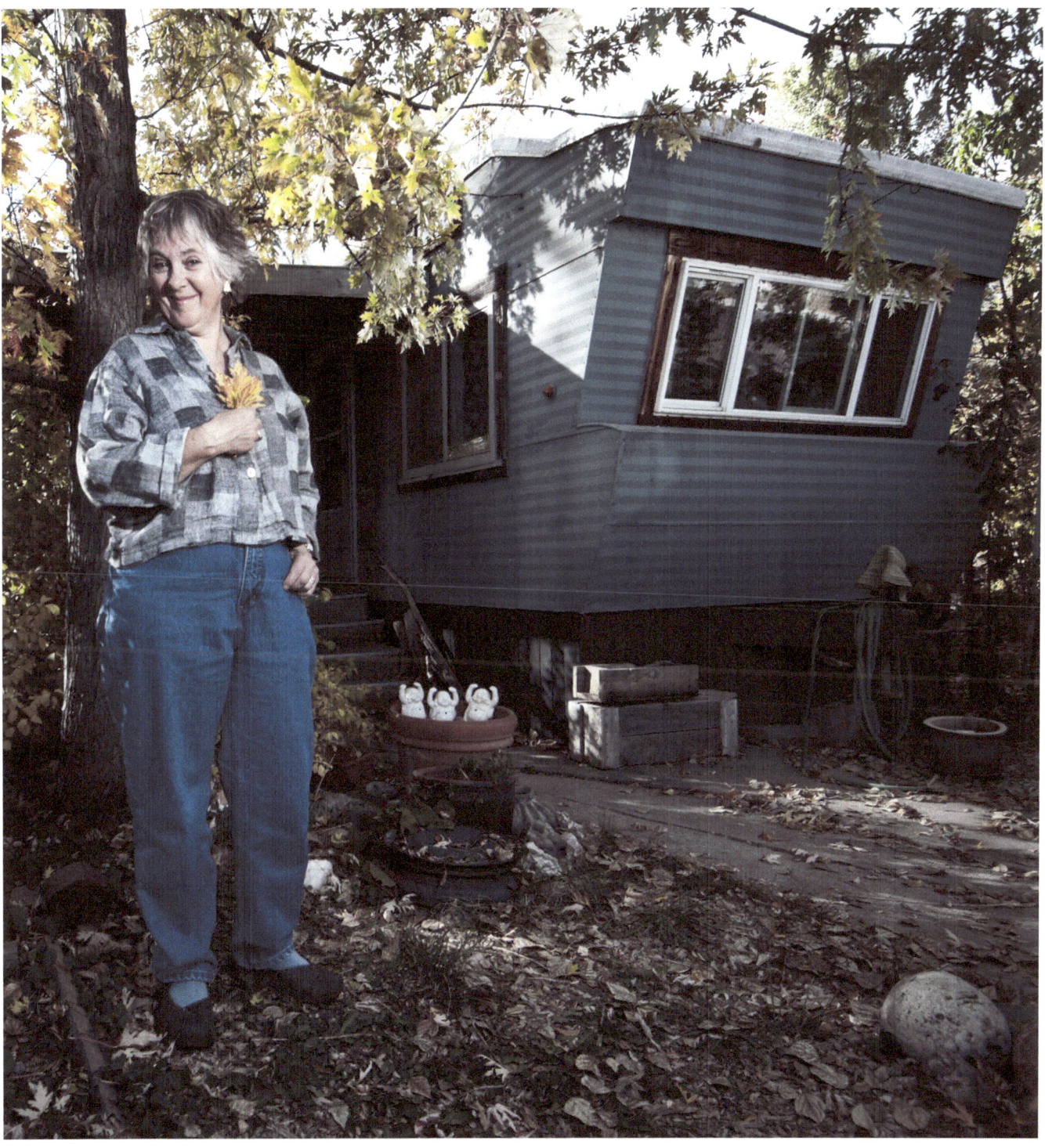

At first it was challenging. I haven't lived in a city in 16 years, just rural places. But now we're fixing the trailer to fit our needs. Everyone's happy, with a little space they call their own. We're able to live here in Boulder, and our kids go to really good schools. We're constantly in touch with each other. It's like a little village.

We have a wood stove outside, a greenhouse in front, chickens, bees and bunnies. My electric bill for seven people is about $80 per month.

I'm poor by choice. I have the resources to get a 9 to 5, but I've chosen to not have such a big footprint on the planet. We've made a choice to always keep it simple, and we truly sustain ourselves here.

-I.

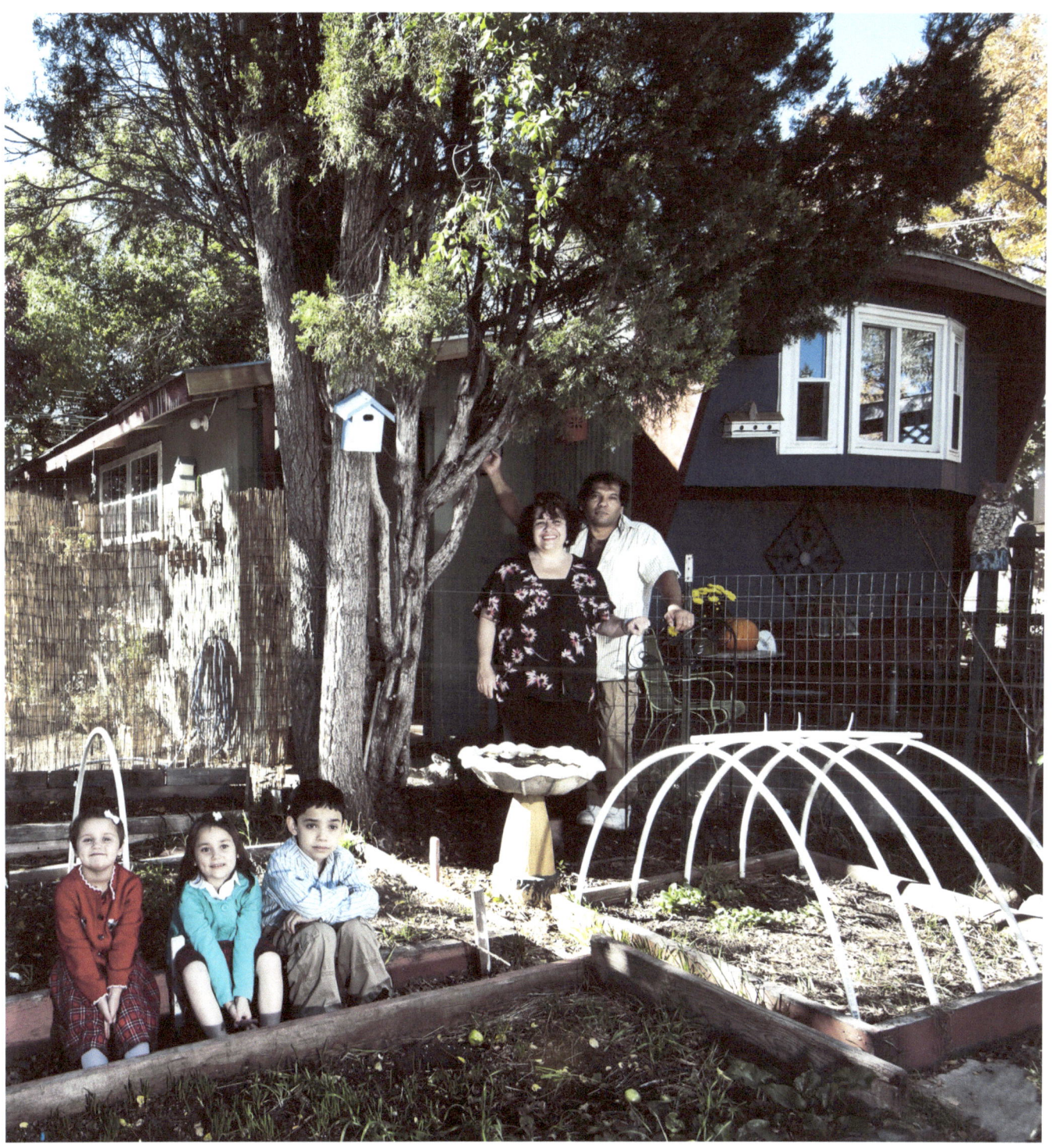

A.- We've lived in the park 7 years.

My first trailer experience was in Findhorn. I thought "this is paradise, this is the perfect place." At night, I could hear the wind. I could hear nature and feel everything around me. For me, trailers have always been an amazing place to live.

When I drive home, driving down the street here, I feel like the luckiest person in the world.

N.- There's such a constant stress to keep it up in society. But here, there's not a lot of pressure to conform. I can really let my personality be visible here in the park.

I still have a little internalized stigma around living in a trailer park. I've never gotten bad feedback. I also haven't told certain people, if I could sense they would judge it.

-A. & N.

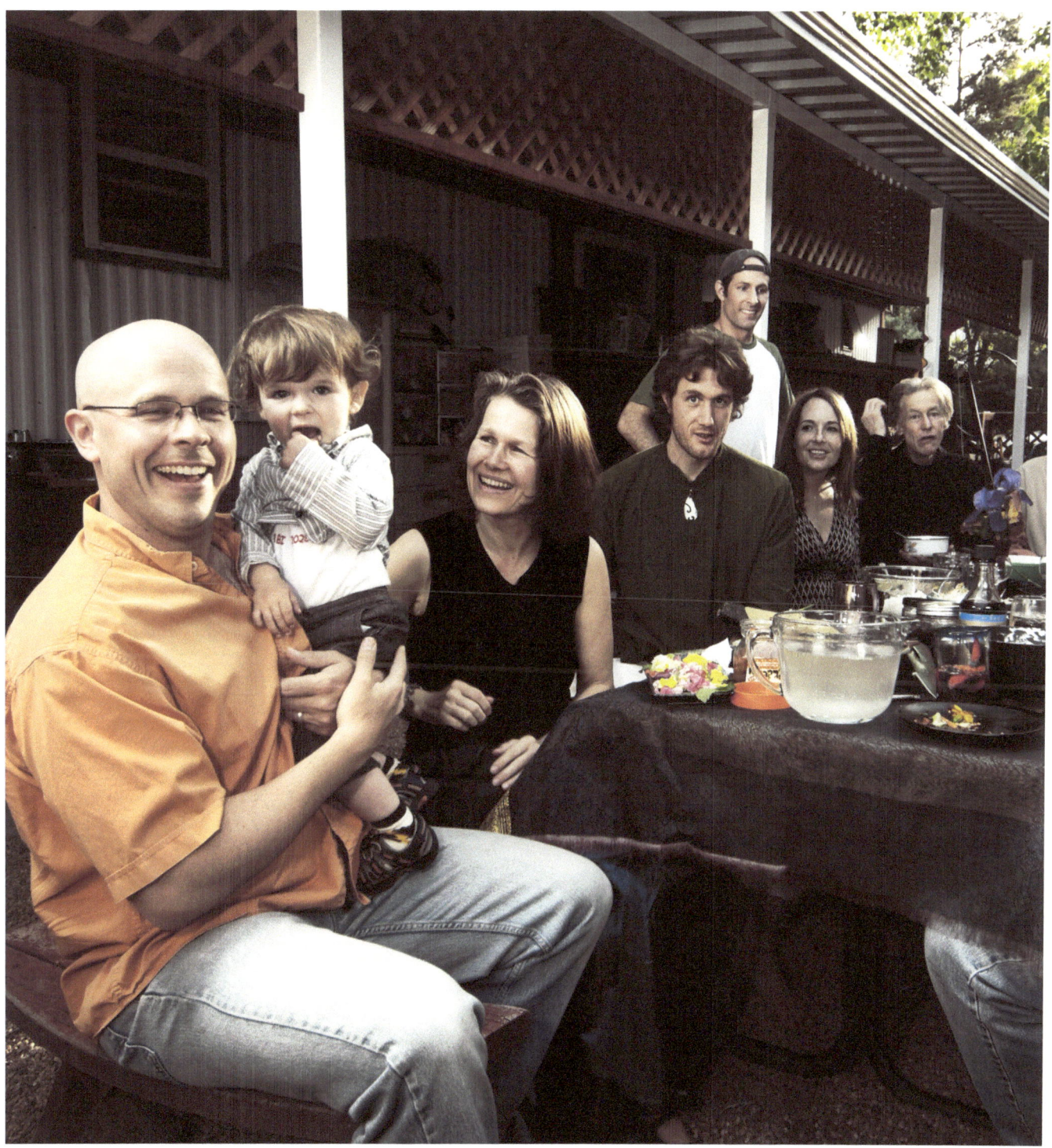

www.ingramcontent.com/pod-product-compliance
Lightning Source LLC
Chambersburg PA
CBHW050803180526
45159CB00004B/1535